Tipbook
Clarinet

The Complete Guide

Hugo Pinksterboer

Tipbook
Clarinet

The Complete Guide

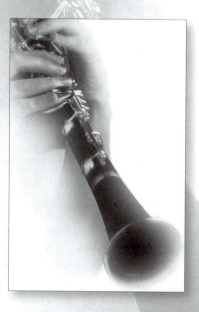

HAL•LEONARD®

The Complete Guide to Your Instrument!

First edition published in 2001 by The Tipbook Company bv,
The Netherlands

Second edition published in 2010 by
Hal Leonard Books
An Imprint of Hal Leonard Corporation
7777 West Bluemound Road
Milwaukee, WI 53213

Trade Book Division Editorial Offices
19 West 21st Street, New York, NY 10010

Printed in the United States

Book design by Gijs Bierenbroodspot

Library of Congress Cataloging-in-Publication Data

Pinksterboer, Hugo.
  Tipbook clarinet : the complete guide / Hugo Pinksterboer.
      p. cm.
  Originally published: Netherlands : Tipbook, 2001.
  Includes bibliographical references and index.
  ISBN 978-1-4234-6524-9 (pbk. : alk. paper)
1. Clarinet. I. Title.
  ML945.P56 2010
  788.6'219--dc22

                                    2010001543

www.halleonard.com

Thanks!

For their information, their expertise, their time, and their help we'd like to thank the following musicians, teachers, technicians and other clarinet experts:

Rose Sperrazza (International Clarinet Association), Terry Landry, François Kloc (Buffet Crampon), James Grondin (Woodwind & Brasswind), Linda and Bill Brannen (Brannen Woodwinds), Mrs. Wurlitzer (Herbert Wurlitzer, Germany), Aaron McEvers, Jerry Hall (Leblanc), Mr. Hammerschmidt (Hammerschmidt, Germany), Erika Block (Backun Musical Services), Dean S. Loy, John Stringer, Herman Braune (Conservatory of Amsterdam), Lute Hoekstra, Walter Boeykens (Conservatories of London, Antwerp, and Rotterdam), Eddy Vanoosthuyse, Gaby Kerrmann and Rupert Naumann (Schreiber, Germany), John de Beer and Coen Wolfgram (NERV: Dutch Single Reed Association), Wouter Bierenbroodspot, Henri Bok (Conservatory of Rotterdam), Rijmert Goppel, Dr. Harm van der Geest, Maarten Jense, Bas de Jong, Koos van Nieuwkasteele, Marianne Poelhekken, Hein Pijnenburg, Henk Rensink, Jos Ruiters, Bert Steinmann, Karin Vrieling (*De Klarinet*), René Wiggers, Pieter Bukkems, Ton Minnen (JT Music), Richard Boerstra, Aad Contze (BIN/Selmer), Piet Jeegers (Piet Jeegers mouthpieces), Frits de Jong (Buffet Crampon), Gerard Koning (Yamaha), Ton Kooiman, Leo van Oostrom, Martin Schaap, Han van Schaik, Casper van der Spek, Frans Philippens (Adams Music Centre), and Robin Bakker (Harry Bakker Saxophones).

We also wish to thank everyone at JIC (Leblanc), Muller, and Yamaha for supplying instruments and further assistance, Maartje Peek for her musical help in making the cover and the Tipcode-movies, and Jelte Althuis for his contribution to the Tipbook clarinet fingering charts.

V

About the Author

Journalist and musician **Hugo Pinksterboer**, author and editor of The Tipbook Series has published hundreds of interviews, articles and instrument reviews, and DVD, CD, and book reviews for a variety of international music magazines.

About the Designer

Illustrator, designer, and musician **Gijs Bierenbroodspot** has worked as an art director for a wide variety of magazines and has developed numerous ad campaigns. While searching in vain for information about saxophone mouthpieces, he got the idea for this series of books on music and musical instruments. He is responsible for the layout and illustrations of all of the Tipbooks.

Acknowledgments

Concept, design, and illustrations: Gijs Bierenbroodspot
Cover photo: René Vervloet
Editor: Robert L. Doerschuk and Meg Clark
Proofreaders: Nancy Bishop and René de Graaff

Anything missing?

Any omissions? Any areas that could be improved? Please go to www.tipbook.com to contact us. Thanks!

Trademarks

Trademarks and/or usernames have been used in this book solely to identify the products or instruments discussed. Such use does not identify endorsement by or affiliation with the trademark owner(s).

Contents

Introduction

Have you just started playing the clarinet? Are you thinking about buying a clarinet, or do you just want to learn more about the one you already have? If so, this book will tell you all you need to know. It covers buying and renting instruments, lessons and practicing, auditioning and selecting a clarinet, choosing mouthpieces, reeds, barrels, and ligatures, as well as maintenance and tuning, the history and the family of the clarinet, and much more.

Having read this Tipbook, you'll be able to get the best out of your instrument, to buy the best clarinet you can, and to easily grasp any other literature on the subject, from books and magazines to catalogs and online publications.

Basics
The first four chapters are meant for beginning players, or their parents. They explain the basics of the instrument and the different clarinet voices, and inform you on learning to play the clarinet, practicing, and buying or renting an instrument. This information also fully prepares you to read the rest of the book.

Advanced players
Advanced players can skip ahead to Chapter 5, where you find everything you need to know to make an informed purchase when you're going to buy a clarinet. Chapters 6 and 7 offer similar

information on selecting mouthpieces, barrels, ligatures, and reeds. Chapter 7 also covers reed adjustment tips.

Maintenance
Chapters 8 and 9 deal with maintenance, from assembly and tuning to cleaning, and related subjects. Tips on buying essential accessories are also included.

Background information
The final chapters offer essential reading material on the history of the clarinet, the family of the instrument, its production, and the main brand names that you'll come across.

US dollars
Please note that all price indications listed on the following pages are based on estimated street prices in American dollars.

Glossary
The glossary at the end of the book briefly explains most of the terms you'll come across as a clarinet player. Also included are an index of terms, and a couple of pages for essential notes on your instrument.

Tipbook fingering charts
Many readers of the first edition of this Tipbook asked us to include fingering charts — and so we did. True: You can find fingering charts on the Internet also, but a book is easier to take along (and you don't have to turn it on either). Besides, the Tipbook Fingering Charts are presented in a very clear way, showing all relevant fingerings for each note on a double page, so you don't have to go back and forth to compare various fingerings. Enjoy!

— Hugo Pinksterboer

See and Hear What You Read with Tipcodes

www.tipbook.com

In addition to the many illustrations on the following pages, Tipbooks offer you a new way to see — and even hear — what you are reading about. The Tipcodes that you will come across regularly in this book give you access to extra pictures, short videos, sound files, and other additional information at www.tipbook.com.

Here's how it works. Below the paragraph on using a whetstone on page 109 is a short section marked **Tipcode CLR-010**. Type in that code on the Tipcode page at www.tipbook.com and you will see a short video that shows you how to adjust the underside of a reed. Similar videos are available on a variety of subjects; other Tipcodes will link to a sound file.

TIPCODE

Tipcode CLR-010
This Tipcode demonstrates two ways to adjust a reed's facing.

XII

Tipbook

Clarinet

The Complete Guide

1

Clarinetists

As a clarinetist you can play in all kinds of groups and orchestras, and in a wide variety of musical styles, from classical music to all kinds of folk music and jazz.

With a clarinet you can play as soft as a whisper, but also loudly enough, as a soloist, to be heard above an entire orchestra. This is just one of the things that make the clarinet such a special instrument. Another is that the clarinet has a remarkable range: It can sound both very low and very high notes — and you can make the instrument sound shy or timid and edgy or brash, or anything in between.

Violins, trumpets, and clarinets
Clarinetists can be heard in so many different musical styles because their instrument blends so well with all kinds of instruments. A clarinet sounds great with the violins in a symphony orchestra, as well as with the trumpets in a concert band, or with many other clarinets in a clarinet choir, for example.

Wind quintets and jazz bands
Clarinets blend well with the piano or the human voice, they're an essential part of a wind quintet (clarinet, oboe, flute, bassoon, and French horn) and often can be heard in jazz. Pretty much all Dixieland jazz bands have a clarinetist, and some modern jazz groups do too. In Chapter 15 you'll find more information about different kinds of groups and orchestras you can join as a clarinetist.

Types of sound
For classical music, clarinetists usually want their instruments to sound dark, warm, and focused. Clarinetists who play outdoors typically go for a louder, 'bigger' tone, while most jazz players favor a brighter, more flexible sound. As a clarinetist, you can do it all. The instrument (and the reed, the mouthpiece and other parts) plays an important role in the sound you produce — but you are the crucial element when it comes to a great, musical tone.

Learning to play
The clarinet is not the very easiest instrument to start on, but with a little talent and half an hour's practice a day you'll be able to play a few standard tunes within only two or three months.

A wide variety
Clarinets come in many different variations. They can be made of wood or plastic; most are nearly black but they're also available

B♭ clarinet
and bass
clarinet.

in bright colors; and they come with all kinds of different mechanisms. This book covers all of those differences in detail, without getting overly technical.

Large and small

Most clarinetists play a so-called soprano clarinet or B-flat (B♭) clarinet, but there are smaller and larger clarinets too. The large bass clarinet, for example, shown on the previous page. It is a good deal bigger, as you can see. The larger size makes the bass clarinet sound much lower than a soprano clarinet. Playing the bass clarinet is not quite the same as simply playing a big clarinet, and clarinetists often specialize in that instrument. All other clarinet sizes or voices are shown in Chapter 11.

2

A Quick Tour

The mechanism or key work of a clarinet make the instrument look more complicated than it really is. This chapter introduces you to the main parts of the clarinet, shedding light on what they're called and what they do.

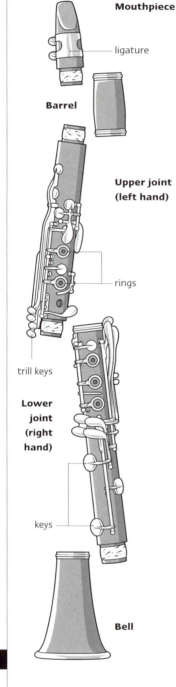

A clarinet consists of five sections.

Mouthpiece

ligature

Barrel

Upper joint (left hand)

rings

trill keys

Lower joint (right hand)

keys

Bell

Essentially, a clarinet is a long tube with holes in it. Similar to a recorder, you play the lowest note by closing all of those *toneholes*. If you open the last hole, the tone goes up. If you then open the next tonehole, the tone goes up some more, and so on.

Finger extensions

The toneholes of a clarinet are too far apart for you to be able to cover them all with your fingers, as you do on a recorder. Besides, there are more toneholes than you have fingers. That's why clarinets have *keys*. This keywork allows you to easily open and close all of the instrument's toneholes.

Five sections

A clarinet consists of five main sections, as shown on to the left. Right at the top is the *mouthpiece* with the *reed*, which is held in place by the *ligature*. When you play the clarinet, you make the reed vibrate. The reed in turn makes the air in the clarinet vibrate — and vibrating air is sound.

Barrel

Under the mouthpiece is the *barrel*, which indeed resembles a barrel. You use it to tune the clarinet, so it's also known as the *tuning barrel*.

Upper joint and lower joint

The two largest sections of the

clarinet are the *upper joint* or *left-hand joint*, which you hold with your left hand when you play, and the *lower joint* or *right-hand joint*.

Thumb rest

The weight of the clarinet rests on your right thumb. On many clarinets, the *thumb rest* can be set a little bit higher or lower, to adjust it to your hands and your technique.

The bell

At the bottom of the lower joint is the *bell*, the widely flaring end of the clarinet.

MECHANISM

The keys and *key rods* or axles are collectively called the *mechanism* or the keywork. It looks rather complicated, but it isn't really.

Your fingers

The mechanism becomes a lot easier to understand if you simply focus on the keys and levers on which you actually put your fingers. They're clearly shown in the illustration on the following pages.

Six rings

Clarinets usually have six *ring keys* or *rings*, five of them at the front of the instrument. The sixth is at the back, by your left thumb.

Tipcode CLR-001
The first Tipcode in this book demonstrates some of the notes that you can play with your right hand and your left hand respectively.

TIPCODE

7

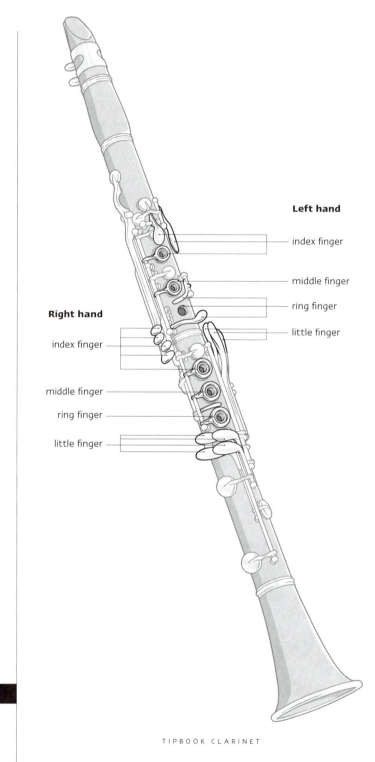

Left hand

index finger

middle finger

ring finger

little finger

Right hand

index finger

middle finger

ring finger

little finger

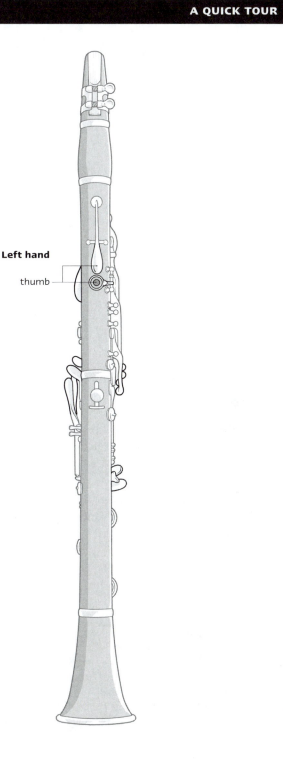

Left hand

thumb

Seventeen keys

Most clarinets have seventeen keys, in addition to those six rings. These instruments are usually indicated as 17/6 clarinets. Some clarinets come with extra keys or rings.

Closed keys

If you have a clarinet handy, you can see that most of the keys are closed, when you are not playing. Take a look at the small keys at the upper side of the instrument, for instance. Small springs make sure they close again when you let go of the lever that operates them.

Open keys

There are only four keys that are open when you are not playing. One is right at the end of the clarinet, close to the bell. When you close that key along with all the others, you play the very lowest note of the instrument, the low E (E3; see page 20).

A fingering chart showing a low B-flat fingering.

Double names

You can use that lowest key to play not just low E, but also a much higher-sounding B. This explains why this key is known as the *E/B key*. Most of the other keys and rings are also used for at least two different notes, so they're often indicated with similar double names.

Fingering charts

Fingering charts are diagrams of the clarinet that show you exactly which keys and toneholes you must close to play a particular note. Fingering charts for the entire range of the clarinet can be found on page 213–229.

THE REGISTERS

On the back of the clarinet is a special key, which you operate with your left thumb. Without this *register key* you can play only a limited number of notes on a clarinet.

Higher register

If you open the register key by pressing it with your left thumb, you are suddenly able to play a whole series of new, higher-sounding notes. In other words, pressing the register key makes you enter a higher *register*.

Chalumeau register

When the register key is closed, you are playing the notes of the bottom register. This is also known as the *chalumeau register*. The lowest note of this register is low E. To play this note, all the toneholes should be closed.

Clarinet register

When you open the register key, you can play all the notes of the higher-sounding *clarinet register*. This register is also known as the *clarion*, *clarino*, or *upper register*. The lowest note of the clarinet register is a B (B4, see page 20). To play this note, all the toneholes should be closed, with the exception of the register key.

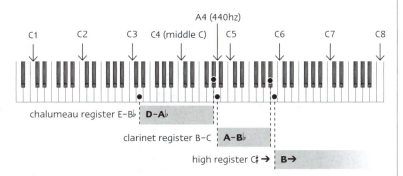

The B♭ clarinet has three registers (displayed in concert pitch).

Tipcode CLR-002
Using the register key, the clarinet produces a note that sounds a twelfth higher. Here are some examples.

TIPCODE

11

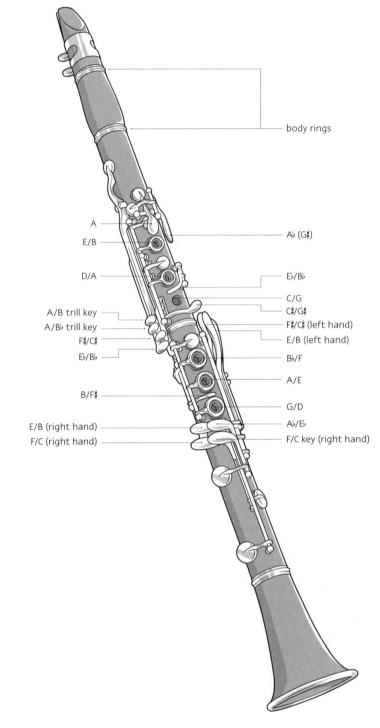

body rings

A

E/B

D/A

A/B trill key

A/B♭ trill key

F#/C#

E♭/B♭

B/F#

E/B (right hand)

F/C (right hand)

A♭ (G#)

E♭/B♭

C/G

C#/G#

F#/C# (left hand)

E/B (left hand)

B♭/F

A/E

G/D

A♭/E♭

F/C key (right hand)

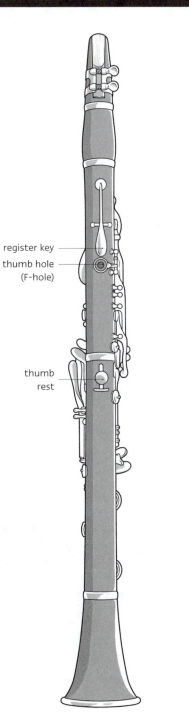

register key

thumb hole
(F-hole)

thumb
rest

Twelfth

On the piano keyboard above you can see that the lowest notes of those two registers (E3 and B4) span twelve white keys. This tonal distance or *interval* is called a *twelfth*.

Other names

That's why the register key is sometimes called the *12th key*: It makes everything sound a twelfth higher. Some clarinetists call it the *speaker key* instead, or the *octave key*. This last name is incorrect (see page 151).

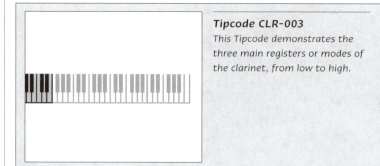

Duodecime

The register key is also known as the **duodecime key**, *based on the Italian name for this interval (duo is two; decime is ten).*

Higher still

The third register of the clarinet is known as the *high register*. The very highest notes (*acute* or *altissimo register*) may easily take a couple of years of practicing.

Modes

The clarinet registers are also referred to as *modes*: the low (chalumeau), middle (clarinet), and high (altissimo) modes.

Tipcode CLR-003
This Tipcode demonstrates the three main registers or modes of the clarinet, from low to high.

14

MORE ABOUT KEYS

Not everybody uses the same names to indicate the keys of the clarinet. For example, some refer to the E/B key as the E key, while others call it the B key.

Open or closed

Likewise, there are clarinetists who name keys or toneholes after the tones that are played when they're closed, while others use the name of the tones played with those keys or toneholes open. That means that the tonehole under your left ring finger is known either as C/G (when closed, as in this book) or as D/A (open).

Numbers

The keys are sometimes numbered instead of using note names — and again, different systems are being used. What one book calls key 5b may be key 12 in another.

Twice the same

Most clarinets have three keys that you can operate with either your left little finger or your right little finger. They are the keys E/B, F/C, and F#/C#. This explains why those key names are shown twice on the illustration on page 12. Which little finger you use for the note will depend mostly on the notes you play just before or just after it.

Trill keys

Your little fingers and index fingers control more than one key each. Your right index finger has no fewer than five keys to operate: one ring key, and the four keys that you press with the side of your finger. Although these side keys are commonly known as *trill keys*, only the upper two are specifically used for playing trills.

Bridge

Under the trill keys you can see the *bridge*. As it connects the rings of the lower joint with the second ring of the upper joint, this mechanism is also known as the *connection* or the *correspondence*.

15

The bridge.

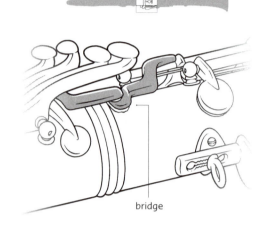

bridge

Pads

Inside every *key cup* is a *pad*. This is a small disc covered with a soft material that ensures that the key seals the tonehole properly, just as your fingertip would: noiseless and airtight. Key cups are also known as *pad cups*.

IN B♭

The most commonly used clarinet is the B♭ clarinet. If you play a C on this clarinet, you hear a B♭, which is exactly one whole step lower than a C. Why is that?

Playing fingerings

If your chart shows Middle C, the note on the first l*edger line* below the staff, you have to close the three toneholes by your left hand. You are then playing a C *fingering*. On a B♭ clarinet, that C fingering will sound a B♭.

C clarinets

Some clarinets are pitched in C instead. If you play a C fingering on one, you'll hear a C. That seems simpler, but there is one

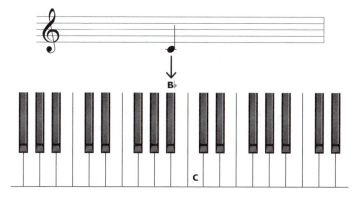

On a B♭ clarinet, a written C sounds the same pitch as a B♭ on the piano.

problem: Being pitched a little higher, a C clarinet is slightly shorter than a B♭ clarinet. The extra length of a B♭ instrument makes it sound just a little warmer, fuller, and darker, and this has been the preferred sound for many, many years. This explains why this clarinet is the most popular choice.

E♭ and A

In many orchestras you will also find the small E♭ clarinet. This sounds a good deal higher and brighter than the B♭ clarinet. Clarinetists in symphony orchestras often use an A clarinet as well as the B♭ clarinet. Being slightly longer, the A instrument sounds a little lower and darker. All other clarinets are listed in Chapter 11.

Transposing instruments

Instruments that are not pitched in C are known as *transposing instruments*. The composer writes *transposed parts* for them.

Write a C, hear E♭

If a composer wants to use the bright sound of an E♭ clarinet, he needs to write a part in E♭. If the tone E♭ is required, that chart will show the note C. You finger a C — simply using the same fingering as on a regular B♭ clarinet! — and the audience hears an E♭. That's all there is to it.

Concert B♭

If you finger a C on a B♭ clarinet, you'll hear a B♭, which is also known as *concert B♭* or *B♭ concert pitch*.

17

The alto clarinet is between the smaller B♭ clarinet and the larger bass clarinet.

ALTO AND BASS CLARINETS

Alto and bass clarinets are popular instruments in various types of orchestras and in clarinet choirs.

Bass
At first sight the bass clarinet looks very different from the soprano. It is a whole lot bigger, and to avoid it becoming too long to handle, it has a curved, metal neck, and a metal bow connecting the bell to the instrument.

Closed hole keys
Also, bass clarinets don't have ring keys or open toneholes, since most of their toneholes are too big to cover with your fingers. Instead, they have *closed-hole keys*, also known as *plateau-style keys* or *covered keys*. Bass clarinets also have more keys that you can operate with your left- and right-hand little fingers. Still, it's basically the same instrument, and it has basically the same keywork.

In B♭
The bass clarinet is usually pitched in B♭. It sounds exactly one octave lower (eight white keys on a piano) than a soprano (B♭) clarinet, when you play the same fingerings.

Alto clarinets
The alto clarinet is somewhere between the soprano clarinet and the bass clarinet. Some alto clarinets have both

closed-hole keys and rings, others have closed-hole keys only. Alto clarinets are pitched in E♭. Using the same fingerings, it sounds a *fifth* (five white keys on a piano) lower than the soprano clarinet, and an octave lower than the soprano clarinet in E♭. All the other clarinets are described in Chapter 11, *The Family*.

HOW HIGH AND HOW LOW

Clarinets have a remarkably large *range*. There's more than three and a half octaves between the highest and the lowest note that you can play on the instrument. The range of a bass clarinet is

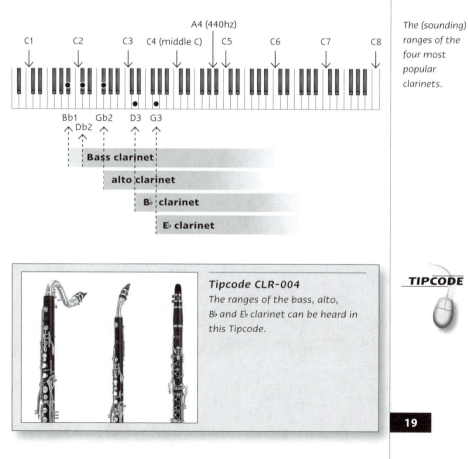

The (sounding) ranges of the four most popular clarinets.

Tipcode CLR-004
The ranges of the bass, alto, B♭ and E♭ clarinet can be heard in this Tipcode.

TIPCODE

even bigger: A good player can span more than four octaves on that instrument.

Seeing and hearing

The piano keyboard on the previous page shows you the impressive ranges of the small E♭ clarinet, the B♭ clarinet, the alto clarinet, and the bass clarinet. These ranges are also demonstrated in Tipcode CLR-004.

THE OCTAVES

When all the keys of the regular B♭ clarinet are closed, you play low E. This is not the only E you can play on a clarinet: You can also play this note one, two and even three octaves higher.

E3–E6

Notes are numbered to identify the octave in which they are played. The lowest E on the clarinet is E3, the highest is E6. Alternatively, you may find indications such as an underscore e (for E3) and e''' (e, three-lined octave; equals E6).

FRENCH AND GERMAN

This Tipbook is mainly about the *French clarinet* or *Boehm clarinet*. There are also German clarinets, which sound and look different. They are mainly used in Germany, but you may come across them in other countries too. There's more about these instruments on page 67 and onwards.

3

Learning to Play

The clarinet is not the hardest instrument to learn to play, but it's not the easiest either. You can master a few basic tunes in a matter of weeks or months, but you can also spend years working on your technique and on developing a beautiful tone — just like with any other instrument.

To make a clarinet sound good, you need to learn a good breathing technique. Playing the clarinet or any other wind instrument involves more than simply blowing a lot of air into it. You will have to learn to support your breath, and to control your air stream. Your teacher will help you!

Embouchure

The way your instrument sounds has a lot to do with how you use your lips, jaws, tongue and all the muscles around them, when you play. Altogether that is known as the *embouchure*.

Mechanism

It doesn't usually take too long to get used to the complex-looking keywork of the instrument. After all, this mechanism was devised to make a clarinet player's life as easy as possible. At first, you will play in the lowest register only. After a few months to a year you'll start using the register key, which means you'll also be playing in the clarinet register. You won't get to the very highest notes for some while longer.

Too young?

The fingers of children below ages ten or eleven are often too thin to stop the toneholes, or too short to reach all of the keys. What's more, the thumbs may not be strong enough to bear the weight of the instrument, which easily weighs some 1½–1¾ pounds (700–800 grams).

Solutions

A neckstrap alleviates the weight problem. You can also start out on a smaller clarinet, such as the E♭ model: There are also special ones with mechanisms made for smaller hands, and even dedicated children's clarinets. Here are some pros, some cons, and some alternatives.

Neckstrap

If you use a neckstrap, the weight of the clarinet is on your neck rather than resting on your thumb only. Straps with a wide, elastic neck band are very popular. The strap is attached to the thumb rest's strap ring. No strap ring? Then attach the strap hook to a

22

short leather strap that you slip over the thumb rest, as shown in the illustration below.

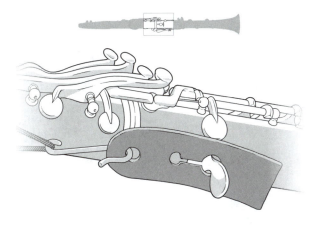

... a leather flap...

Smaller clarinet

A neckstrap won't help you if your fingers are too thin or too short. If this is a problem, some teachers will advise you to start on the smaller E♭ clarinet. However, this means that you have to adapt to playing the larger B♭ clarinet later on. Also, E♭ clarinets are more expensive than B♭ instruments of similar quality.

Other solutions

- The **Kinder Klari** is an affordable E♭ clarinet designed with children in mind. The eleven key instrument is about a third lighter than a regular clarinet, and forty percent smaller.

- Some companies make B♭ clarinets that have **plateau-style keys** (i.e., closed-hole keys) rather then the traditional rings, allowing children with smaller fingers to effectively stop those toneholes.

- The British **Clarinova**, successor of the Lyons clarinet, is aimed at children aged from five or six. With its plastic mechanism, this C clarinet looks very different. It weighs only one third of a regular clarinet, it has extra-small toneholes, all the keys are set extra close together, it needs less maintenance, and is more durable.

23

The light-
weight
Clarinova
(right) and the
Jupiter
Saxonett.

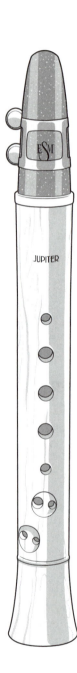

- The very affordable keyless **Saxonett** looks much like a recorder with a clarinet or saxophone mouthpiece.

LESSONS

If you take clarinet lessons, you'll learn about everything connected with playing the clarinet, from breathing and embouchure to playing in tune, and from reading music to good posture.

Finding a teacher

Looking for a private teacher? Larger music stores may have teachers on staff, or they can refer you to one, and some players have found great teachers in musicians they have seen in performance. You can also find teachers online (see page 212). Alternatively, you may consult your local Musicians' Union, ask the band director at a high school in your vicinity, or check the classified ads in newspapers or music magazines. Professional private teachers will usually charge between thirty-five and seventy-five dollars per hour. Some make house calls, for which you'll pay extra.

Group or individual lessons

Instead of taking individual lessons, you can also go for group lessons if that's an option in your vicinity. Private lessons are more expensive, but can be tailored exactly to your needs.

Collectives

You also may want to check whether there are any teachers' collectives or music schools in your vicinity. These collectives may offer extras such as ensemble playing, master classes, and clinics, in a wide variety of styles, and at various levels.

Questions

On your first visit to a teacher, don't simply ask how much it costs. Here are some other questions.

25

- Is an **introductory lesson** included? This is a good way to find out how well you get on with the teacher, and, for that matter, with the instrument.

- Is the teacher interested in taking you on as a student if you are just doing it **for the fun of it**, or are you expected to practice at least three hours a day?

- Do you have to make a large investment in method books right away, or is **course material provided**?

- Can you **record your lessons**, so that you can listen at home to how you sound, and once more to what's been said?

- Are you allowed to fully concentrate on the **style of music you want to play**, or will you be required to learn other styles? Or will you be stimulated to do so?

- Is this teacher going to make you **practice scales** for two years, or will you be pushed onto a stage as soon as possible?

Non-classical

Because clarinetists mainly play classical music, many clarinet teachers tend to give 'classical' lessons. Of course, some teachers are equally well at home in other musical styles, if not more so.

PRACTICING

What goes for every instrument goes especially for wind instruments: It's better to practice half an hour every day than a whole day once a week. This is especially true for your embouchure: If you don't play for a few days, you'll feel it immediately.

Three times ten

How long should you practice? That depends on your talent and on what you want to achieve. As an indication: Half an hour a day usually results in steady progress. If playing half an hour at a stretch seems too long, try dividing it up into two quarter-hour sessions, or three of ten minutes each.

> ### Setting goals
> *Rather than focusing on how long you need to practice, it may be wise to set a goal for each practice session, or for the next week. That allows you to focus on the music, rather than on the clock! For more information on this approach and a host of other tips on practicing, please check out Chapter 15.*

TIP

In tune
Practice is also important for learning to play your instrument musically, which certainly involves playing in tune. The longer you play, and the better you learn to listen to yourself, the easier it will be to get each note perfectly in tune.

Neighbors
There are few instruments you can play as softly as a clarinet, but of course you won't always. If neighbors or housemates are bothered by your playing, it may be enough to simply agree to fixed practice times. If you really play a lot, it may be better to insulate a room. Even a very large cupboard can be big enough. There are books available on sound insulation, you can ask around to find people who sound-proofed a room, or you can hire a specialized contractor to do the job. Of course, it may be easier to find a place that works a little better for practicing.

On CD
Playing the clarinet is something you usually do in a group, so it's often more fun to practice 'together' too — even if there aren't any other musicians around. There are all kinds of CDs available to play along to, in all kinds of styles, for beginners as well as for more advanced clarinetists. Your own part is left off, leaving the other musicians for you to play with.

Computer lessons
If you have a computer handy, you can also use special CD-ROMs to practice with. Some feature entire orchestras: You can decide for yourself how fast you want a piece to be played, and which parts

27

you want to hear. There is also software that allows you to slow down difficult phrases on a recording, so you can find out what's going on at your own tempo.

Metronome

Most pieces of music are supposed to be played just as fast at the end as at the beginning. Playing with a metronome helps you to achieve this. A metronome is a small mechanical or electronic device that ticks or bleeps out a steady adjustable pulse, so you can tell immediately if you're dragging or speeding.

Two mechanical metronomes and two electronic ones.

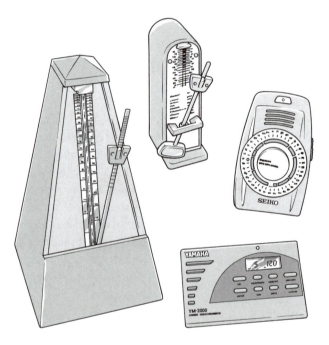

Listen and play

Learning to play the instrument is not about practicing only; it's also about listening to music. So visit festivals, concerts, and other performances. Go listen to orchestras, wind quartets, and other ensembles, in any style of music. One of the best ways to learn to play is seeing other musicians at work. Living legends or local amateurs — every concert's a learning experience. And the best way to learn to play? Play a lot!

Record your practice sessions

No matter how good you are, it's always hard to judge your own playing as you play. Tip: record your practice sessions, or your first or subsequent attempts to play the piece that you have been practicing, and then judge your performance by listening to the recording, once or a couple of times. This is very instructive for musicians at any level.

Also consider recording your lessons, so you can listen once more to what was said, and especially to how you sounded, when you get home. All you need is a portable recording device with a built-in microphone. A computer is great for home recording!

4

Buying A Clarinet

You can buy a new clarinet for as little as three or four hundred dollars. The most expensive clarinets cost ten times as much, if not more. Of course you can rent one first, to find out whether the instrument suits you. Or you can buy one secondhand. This chapter has all the information you'll need to help you make a decision when purchasing a clarinet.

The most affordable clarinets are made of plastic. They usually come with a case and a mouthpiece, and often one or two reeds are included as well. Contrary to wooden instrument, plastic clarinets cannot crack. They also weigh less and need less maintenance — important characteristics for student instruments. Prices start below two hundred dollars, but there are eight or nine hundred dollar plastic clarinets as well.

Wood

In most stores, wooden clarinets start around seven or eight hundred dollars, typically providing you with a more musical, warmer tone. The mechanism of these instruments also makes them easier to play, last longer, and require less adjustment. Do note that plastic clarinets in this price range also offer those mechanic qualities.

Mid-range

Intermediate clarinetists often spend one to two thousand dollars when buying a new instrument. That extra money buys you a clarinet that usually has better intonation, sounds bettter, and is easier to play, because better materials have been used and more care has been devoted to its construction. It's not always easy to tell a higher-priced instrument from its appearance. One simple reason is that even the most affordable instruments often look great, especially to the untrained eye.

Professional

Most advanced and professional players use instruments that cost over two thousand dollars. The more you spend, the harder it becomes to hear or see the differences between one instrument and the other, and you need to be a good player to bring out

TIP

For beginners

For obvious reasons, most beginners start on low-budget instruments. Do note, however, that higher quality instruments are typically easier to play — so investing a little more may be a wise decision.

32

and appreciate those subtleties. The most expensive B♭ clarinets are around five to six thousand dollars.

Other clarinets

The other clarinet voices are more expensive, some because they're bigger, and also because fewer of them are made. For example, E♭ clarinets are smaller than B♭ clarinets, but they often cost a little more. Also, only few companies make low-budget E♭ clarinets. Soprano clarinets in other tunings (e.g., A, C or D) are not available in the very lowest price ranges, and their prices are usually higher than what you'd pay for a B♭ clarinet of similar quality.

Bass clarinets

Plastic bass clarinet start around fifteen hundred dollars, while professional instruments easily cost six or more times as much. The most expensive clarinets, such as professional quality contra bass clarinets, have price tags of thirty thousand dollars and up.

THE SHOP

A clarinet is a precision instrument that needs to be properly maintained and adjusted. It also needs a full overhaul now and again. That's why you're usually best off buying your instrument in a shop that has a clarinet technician on staff. Then you know that they know what they are doing, and that they probably won't send you home with a lousy, badly adjusted instrument. Even new

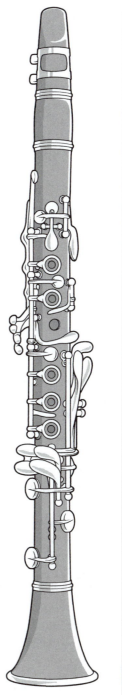

An E♭ clarinet.

clarinets may need to be checked and adjusted one more time before they play well.

Cleaning, oiling, adjusting

Every clarinet needs to be checked and readjusted from time to time (COA: cleaning, oiling, adjusting). If you have bought a new instrument, that service may be free the first time, or for the first year. Some shops and technicians may even send you a reminder when it's time for a COA.

TIP

Another store

When you're going to buy an instrument, it can't do any harm to visit a few different stores or clarinet workshops, because every store has its own sound, and you'll hear different stories and opinions depending on where you go. What's more, not all stores stock all the brands.

Time and space

The more clarinets there are to choose from, the harder the choice can be — but the better your chances of finding exactly the clarinet you're looking for. Be sure to take your time, and remember that it's better to come back another time than to play an hour or longer at a stretch. Stores may have isolated booths for auditioning instruments, so that you don't bother the other customers, or vice versa. Note that such booths may have very dry acoustics.

On approval

Some stores allow you to take an instrument on approval, so that you can assess it at your leisure, both at home and in rehearsals or performances. This is more common with pro-level instruments than with low-budget ones, and you are more likely to be offered this opportunity if you're a good player than if you are choosing your first clarinet. One of the main advantages of trying our a clarinet this way is that you can play it in situations where you know what your current instrument sounds like.

34

Not the same

Even two 'identical' clarinets will never sound exactly the same. So always buy the instrument you thought sounded best, and not an 'identical' one from the stockroom. The same goes for mouthpieces and other parts.

Another clarinetist

In order to hear the differences between one clarinet and another, you need to be able to play well. This is a problem if you're going to buy your first instrument, of course — so take someone with you who can play, or find stores where someone on the staff can.

TIP

Buying online

You can also buy musical instruments online or by mail-order. This makes it impossible to compare instruments (see page 74), but most online and mail-order companies offer a return service for most or all of their products: If you're not happy with it, you can send it back within a certain period of time. Of course the instrument should be in new condition when you send it back.

RENTING

Rather than buying a clarinet, you can rent one. Usually, there's a minimum rental period – three months, for instance, or a school year. The rental fee is usually set as a percentage of the retail price of the instrument. Expect to pay around twenty-five to fifty dollars a month.

The basics

It is impossible to provide a detailed description of the infinite amount of different plans, terms, and conditions you will likely encounter when you decide to rent an instrument. But here are the basics:

35

- Many rental plans are actually **rent-to-own plans**: The instrument is yours once the periodic payments you've made equals the list price. Note that this list price will usually be higher than what you would have paid had you just bought the instrument outright — which explains why most of these plans are interest free.

- Most of these rent-to-own or **hire-purchase plans** also have an option to buy the instrument before you're fully paid up; if you choose to buy the instrument, your rent paid to date will usually be applied to the instrument.

- With a **lease plan** — also known as a straight rental plan or rent-to-rent plan — you simply keep paying rent until you return the instrument. Rates are usually lower on these plans than those of rent-to-own plans. With these plans, renting for a long period of time will be, of course, more expensive than buying the instrument.

Maintenance and insurance

Maintenance is usually included in the rental fee, but some plans offer it as a separate expense. The main thing is to make sure you don't have to worry about it. Insurance may be included as well. Make sure you understand what is and isn't covered under your lease or rental plan.

- Does the fee **include** instrument set-up, maintenance, and finance or bank charges?

- If **insurance** is included, does it also cover theft and loss?

- Do you get a **replacement** instrument if yours needs maintenance?

- Do you have to pay an origination fee, an application fee, or a deposit? These **fees** are usually non-refundable; they often may be applied to the rental, however.

- Always ask if you get a **new or a used** (rental-return) instrument.

- Is there a **reconditioning fee**, a stocking fee, or a depreciation fee when you return the instrument?

• Note that stores may ask for a **deposit** or require your credit card details.

PRE-OWNED INSTRUMENTS

Buying a pre-owned instrument may allow you to buy a higher quality instrument than you can when buying new. And if you take proper care of your investment, you may be able to sell it for a similar price once you're ready for a higher quality clarinet.

Privately or in a store?
Purchasing a pre-owned instrument from a private party may be cheaper than buying an identical instrument from a store. Buying in a store has its advantages, though. Stores typically sell instruments that have been checked and adjusted, you can go back if you have questions, and stores may offer you a limited warranty on your purchase. Another difference is that a good dealer won't usually ask an outrageous price. Private sellers might, either because they don't know any better, or because they think you don't.

A second opinion
If you go to buy a used clarinet, it's even more important to take along an advanced player who knows about the instrument — especially if you're going to buy privately. Otherwise you might turn down a decent clarinet just because it doesn't look good, or get saddled with an instrument that looks great but doesn't sound good or doesn't have good intonation, making it harder to play in

TIP

> **Appraisal**
> If you want to be sure you're not paying too much, get the instrument appraised first. A knowledgeable clarinet technician can tell you exactly what a used clarinet is worth, whether it needs any work done, and what the extra work costs.

37

tune. Technical tips for buying pre-owned instruments begin on page 77.

Sieve

Many decent clarinets in disrepair can be made to sound good, even if they leak like a sieve and you can barely get a sound out of them. If you buy an instrument in this condition, you should be aware that it can easily cost you hundreds of dollars to get it fixed.

AND FINALLY

What you consider the best clarinet may well be the one your favorite clarinetist plays. Does that mean you should buy the same instrument? There isn't much point. Even if you use exactly the same clarinet, the same mouthpiece, and the same reed, you'll still sound different.

One on two, two on one

If you get a clarinetist to play two different clarinets, you're likely to hear little difference. But two different clarinetists on the same instrument won't sound the same at all. In other words: The sound depends more on the player than on the instrument or any of its parts.

The same

Even so, you often see all clarinetists in an orchestra playing the same clarinet (they often have to), and even using the same type of mouthpiece. This helps the clarinet section to sound as a whole, rather than as a number of clarinetists. That said, you're likely to sound better or play much easier on a different mouthpiece than your fellow clarinetists.

Brochures and online sources

If you want to be well informed before you go out to buy or rent an instrument, get hold of as many clarinet brochures and catalogs as you can find, along with the price lists, and check out the websites of clarinet makers and other online sources.

Books and magazines

Additionally, there are several other books on the subject, as well as various magazines that offer reviews and other articles on the instrument, and on reeds, mouthpieces and related products. Titles, addresses and other information on additional resources can be found on pages 209–212.

Conventions and workshops

All kinds of get-togethers are organized for clarinetists, from clarinet conventions and courses to workshops and demonstrations. You can find out more about your instrument there, and you'll always learn something from the other clarinetists you meet.

5

A Good Instrument

Even if you take a closer look, it may be hard to see the differences between one soprano clarinet and the other. They're all the same shape and size, they're usually all black, and all the keys, rings and holes are in the same places. Yet one may cost five or ten times as much as the next, one can sound much better, and another may be much easier to play. This chapter tells you more about the visible and invisible differences between clarinets, and provides handy tips for auditioning clarinets.

More than anything else, the sound of a clarinet depends on you: A good clarinetist can make even a student instrument sound impressive. Next in importance are the reed, the mouthpiece, and the barrel; all three are discussed separately in Chapters 6 and 7.

Different sounds

There are all kinds of reasons why clarinets can sound and play so differently. This chapter begins with the different materials the instrument can be made of, followed by important topics such as the bore (the shape of the inside of the instrument), the toneholes (page 51), the mechanism (page 55), extra keys and the full Boehm clarinet (62), and German clarinets (67). A section on pre-owned instruments is also included.

With your ears

If you prefer to select a clarinet using your ears alone, then go straight to the tips for auditioning instruments, beginning on page 73.

All the same

Clarinetists rarely agree about anything. The following chapters won't tell you who is right, or what is best, but rather what various experts think about different issues. You'll only discover who you agree with by playing and by listening to as many clarinets and clarinetists as you can.

All clarinets

This book is mainly about the B♭ clarinet, but most of what you read here also applies to all other clarinets as well.

MATERIALS

Student clarinets are typically made of plastic; more expensive ones are made of wood, and some companies offer an in-between solution with wooden clarinets that have a plastic bell. What are the differences?

Plastic: the advantages

Plastic clarinets have many advantages. They are less expensive, can't crack, need less maintenance, and weigh considerably less (about a quarter of a pound, or 100 grams) than wooden instruments. This is especially good news for children.

Playing outdoors

Plastic clarinets are also better resistant to rain or sunshine, and they're insensitive to changes in air humidity or temperature; you don't have to keep retuning them when it gets colder or hotter either. This is why they are often used for outdoor playing.

Preferably wood

Even so, most clarinetists prefer to play wooden instruments, as they usually sound richer, darker, and warmer. That's certainly not all because of the material: The main reason why wooden clarinets tend to sound better is simply that clarinet makers use wood to make their better instruments. There are no professional plastic clarinets.

Looks

Most plastic clarinets are easy to recognize, usually because of their shinier, solid black look. Not al plastic instruments look that way. Some use plastics that look a little like wood (i.e., *wood-grained polymers*), or they have a matte or a little less smooth (*brushed*) surface. Colored clarinets, in bright yellow, red, blue, or other colors, are also available.

> ### Attractive names
> Because the word 'plastic' has a cheap sound to it, most
> manufacturers come up with a more attractive name for
> the material they use, such as Resotone, Resonite, Sonority
> Resin, or Grena 2000. Plastic clarinets are also referred to as
> composite, resin, or synthetic clarinets.

Only the barrel and the bell

Some otherwise wooden clarinets have a plastic bell. Why? To

43

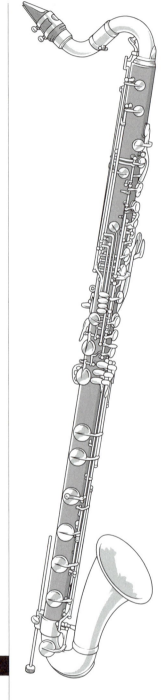

Larger clarinets — such as this bass clarinet, which extends to low C — have a metal neck, bow, and bell.

make a wooden bell, you need a fair-sized chunk of expensive wood. Some of these instruments have a plastic barrel too. The sound of the instrument will often audibly improve if you replace the plastic barrel with a wooden one. Replacing the bell has a similar effect, though it will be less dramatic.

Wooden clarinets

Most wooden clarinets are made of an African wood variety that is extremely hard, heavy, and very dark, almost black in color. It is usually called grenadilla, although you may come across other names, such as African blackwood, m'pingo, and ebony, or the official name, *Dalbergia melanoxylon*. The French company Buffet also makes clarinets from a mixture of (mainly) resin and compressed grenadilla powder.

Other kinds of wood

Less common, but sometimes also used for clarinets is West Indian ebony. This type of wood is also known as *Brya ebenus*, cocuswood, or granadilla. Rosewood, a reddish-brown wood that is said to give a lighter, softer or sweeter tone, is rarer still. There's also a US company that makes hard rubber clarinets. This natural material doesn't crack and is said to make for high quality instruments.

Breaking it in

In order to prevent a new wooden

clarinet from cracking, it's best to break it in carefully. That way the wood, which has been dried in the factory, gets used to the moisture you blow into the instrument.

Various approaches
There are various approaches to how you should break in your instrument. One would be to play it for fifteen minutes every day for the first week, and fifteen minutes per day longer every following week. Others start playing their new instrument five minutes the first day, and add five more every day, or they play no more than half an hour a day for the first month, for example.

Color
Some brands give all their wooden clarinets an extra dark hue by staining them. Other brands don't color them, and some brands offer staining as an option. There is no audible difference.

Metal parts
Larger clarinets, such as the alto and the bass, have metal *necks* instead of barrels. The bell is just about always made of metal too, as is the bow that joins it to the instrument.

Metal clarinets
In Turkish, Greek, and other international folk music groups, you may still find soprano clarinets made entirely of metal. You'd expect them to sound very different from wooden or plastic clarinets, but in fact the difference is barely audible (if you want to know why, please check out page 47). Metal clarinets are a lot lighter, because their walls are very thin.

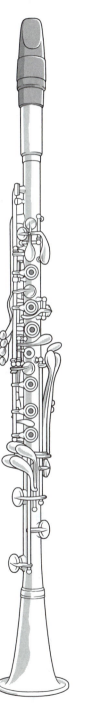

A single-walled metal clarinet.

45

TIP

Single and double walls

Single- and double-wall clarinets have been made and played in the US and Europe too, including instruments from companies such as Conn — with gold-plated keys on a silver body – and Leblanc.

THE BORE

Clarinet makers always state the diameter of the inside of the tube — the *bore* — for each clarinet. The dimensions of the bore have a major effect on how an instrument sounds and plays.

Large or small

Most clarinets have a bore of between 0.577" and 0.585" (14.65–14.85 mm), measured halfway up the instrument. The difference between these 'small' and 'large' bores may not look like much on paper, but they are when you play the instrument.

Wide

Clarinets with a really large bore (up to 0.591"/15 mm) are mostly used by beginners, because they respond more easily. Jazz clarinetists are also likely to chose this type of bore. Though it requires more air, it gives you the volume you often need for playing jazz, and a sound that is usually described as big and open.

Small bore

For a darker, warmer and more subdued, classical type of sound, you'll probably choose an instrument with a smaller bore diameter and a greater blowing resistance.

Different country, different bore

The preferred bore size also varies per country. Clarinetists in France usually go for a small bore; in Austria they prefer a large bore, and most US clarinetists tend to prefer an instrument with a medium size bore. German clarinets come with both small and large bores.

46

Inches to millimeters

Bore sizes are usually stated in inches. To convert to millimeters, multiply that size by 25.4. So for example, a 0.575" bore is 0.575 x 25.4 = 14.60 mm.

Cylindrical

The bore of a clarinet is the same diameter along the greater part of its length: Clarinets have a largely *cylindrical* bore. At certain points, though, the bore diameter becomes smaller, or larger.

Air column

The exact shape of the bore is very important for how a clarinet plays and sounds. Why? When you blow, the reed makes the air in the clarinet vibrate, and vibrating air is sound. In other words, this vibrating air column 'makes' the sound of the clarinet. The character of a clarinet's sound depends to a very large extent on the shape of the air column — and that shape is of course the same as the shape of the bore.

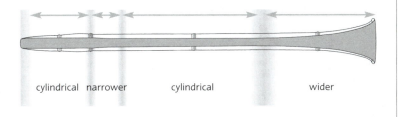

cylindrical   narrower   cylindrical   wider

The shape of the air column is essential for the character of the sound.

The dimensions

The fact that the dimensions of the bore are so important helps explain why metal clarinets don't sound that much different compared to wooden instruments — or even plastic clarinets, should they be made according to the same quality standards and with the same precise dimensions as their wooden counterparts.

TIP

Conical

The bore becomes steadily larger towards the end of the instrument.

47

This *conical* section usually begins somewhere about halfway down the lower joint, and is of course most pronounced at the bell.

Reverse cone

At the top of the upper joint of the clarinet, the bore usually gets smaller by an almost invisible amount (*reverse cone* or *reversing cone*). This produces some extra resistance, and it makes the sound a little darker, warmer, deeper, or more colorful.

Bright and open

A clarinet with an upper joint that doesn't get any smaller, or does so only by a very small amount, usually blows very easily, having a rather bright, open sound — just like an instrument with a large bore. For a somewhat warmer, more focused tone, you may try an instrument with a tapered bore.

Different names

Because this narrowing at the top is so important, all kinds of terms are used to describe that small section. For instance, a *linear cone* means that the tube becomes larger evenly, while *dual taper* indicates that it does so in two steps (first rapidly, then a little more gradually, or the other way around). Many instruments have a *polycylindrical* or a *polyconical bore*, i.e., a bore that narrows in three or more steps.

Sound

All of that jargon is only really important to clarinet makers and technicians, rather than to clarinetists. After all, you don't buy a clarinet because it has a particular bore but because of the way it plays and sounds. That's why most makers also explain the characteristics of the various bore types of their instruments, from more volume to a tone that is easier to control, or a richer sound. Check out clarinet brochures and clarinet makers' websites for such information.

Smooth

A look through the lower joint and upper joint of your clarinet tells you how smoothly the bore has been finished. A smooth bore allows an instrument to sound easier and literally smoother. If a pre-owned clarinet has a really messy-looking bore, that may be because it hasn't been kept clean properly.

Wall thickness

Some clarinets have thicker walls than others. A thicker wall is said to give a thicker, more robust sound that carries further (*projection*). An thin-walled instrument usually responds better and sounds lighter, sweeter, and less penetrating.

Big clarinets

The larger clarinet voices have bigger bores. Alto clarinets, for example, usually have a bore of between 0.670" and 0.710" (17–18 mm), and bass clarinets are between 0.905" and 0.945" (23–24 mm). The smaller E♭ clarinets typically has a bore of around 0.530" (13.5 mm).

THE BELL

The bell is more important to the sound than you might think. It doesn't just influence the sound of the *long-tube notes*, which you play with all or almost all of the toneholes closed, but also the notes that sound from the middle section of the clarinet. Without the bell, your instrument sounds much less resonant than it does with the bell attached.

Try it out

It follows that a clarinet may sound slightly different with one bell than with another. A bell with a wider flare can open up the sound a little, for instance, and a bell with a slightly thicker wall can make for a slightly 'thicker,' darker sound. To be able to hear those differences you need to be a competent musician and have a good instrument. If so, it can really be worthwhile to experiment with different bells. Also check out the section on barrels on pages 94–97. Quite a few small companies specialize in custom made bells and barrels, as these parts can have similar effects to the sound of your instrument.

49

Position

Some clarinetists with very good ears even carefully rotate the bell until they've found the position in which it makes the instrument sound its very best.

For sale separately

Bells are sold separately, not only to improve the sound of the instrument, but also to replace a broken bell. Standard replacement bells soon cost around fifty dollars or more. Special bells can be a lot more expensive; exclusive wooden bass clarinet bells may cost a thousand dollars or more.

TIP

> ### Plastic or wood
>
> *Some plastic student clarinets come with a optional wooden bell, replacing the standard plastic bell. The wooden bell may cost you some ten to fifteen percent extra. If possible, check out the difference in sound this creates!*

Bell ring

Because thin wooden bells are especially vulnerable, they usually have metal *bell rings*. Plastic clarinets have bell rings only for show, and some brands allow you to choose between an instrument with or without a ring. A bell ring makes the instrument a tiny bit heavier. *Tip:* On wooden instruments especially, rings can come loose and cause buzzes.

BODY RINGS AND TENON RINGS

Most clarinets have metal *body rings* wherever two joints meet. These rings, also known as *joint rings* or *ferrules*, are said to influence the sound a bit, restricting the vibrations of the instrument. This is why some clarinets have only very thin body rings or none at all. Do note that it's quite hard to hear this subtle difference.

Tenon rings

The cork-covered ends of the upper and lower joints are the *tenons*. They are often reinforced with metal *tenon rings*. On lower budget clarinets, not every tenon has a ring.

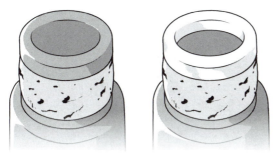

A tenon without, and one with a tenon ring.

Too thick

Always check how easily the barrel, lower joint, upper joint, and bell fit together, and make sure to apply a little cork grease before you do. If the sections slide too easily, there's a chance that air will leak. If they're very hard to assemble, the tenon(s) may need to have a bit of the cork removed. A tip: Assembling a new clarinet will always be a little harder, as the tenons are quite thick. They will get a bit thinner after a while.

TONEHOLES

Clarinets have three kinds of toneholes: Some toneholes have closed keys, others have ring keys, and a few are just open holes. The toneholes that have closed keys are slightly recessed (countersunk) and have beveled edges, which helps the pads to seal the holes properly.

Rings

The toneholes with rings have a small 'chimney.' On some clarinets these toneholes have plastic or hard rubber inserts that are often said to give a brighter sound and be less likely to crack or

51

deform. Other instruments have *integral toneholes*, meaning that the toneholes and the joint they're in are the same piece of wood (see page 156).

The ring key fits around the chimney.

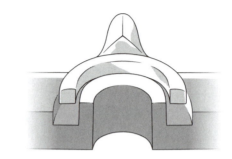

Raised tonehole

The tonehole under the left ring finger really is just a hole, without a ring or a key. On some clarinets this tonehole is raised, bringing its edge up to the same level as the rings so that all of your fingers go down the same distance.

A raised C/G tonehole (Selmer).

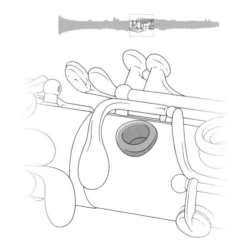

Register tube

If you look through the upper joint of a clarinet, you will see two small metal tubes or sleeves: the *register tube* or *speaker tube* inside the register key's tonehole, and another tube inside the thumbhole. These tubes stop the moisture you blow into your clarinet from running out through those holes. They also affect the sound of an instrument and its *intonation* (how well in tune it is). That's why German clarinets have a register tube too, even though the corresponding tonehole is positioned at the front side of the tube, where it can't get waterlogged.

Gold

Some clarinets come with gold-plated register and speaker tubes. This plating is said to help prevent condensation.

TIP

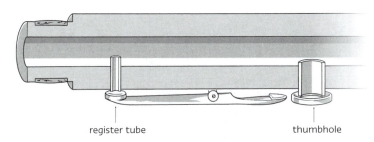

The long, narrow register tube and the shorter tube in the thumbhole.

register tube   thumbhole

Undercut

Most clarinets have *undercut toneholes*, which means every tonehole gets slightly larger at the bottom. Undercut toneholes may improve an instrument's tone, its response, its intonation, and much more: It makes it sound and play better, in other words. If your instrument has straight toneholes — you only really find such toneholes on low budget clarinets — it's harder to adjust the exact pitch of your notes. This actually makes things easier for beginners, since it helps to prevent pitch fluctuations.

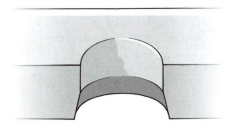

An undercut tonehole

53

Vent holes

Some clarinets have extra holes to make particular notes sound better or more in tune. These *resonance holes* or *vent holes* may be open, or they may have keys (see pages 63–64).

Tuning

Most orchestras, ensembles, and other groups tune to *concert A* (A4; see page 11). If you play this A on a piano, the piano strings vibrate 440 times per second, usually indicated as A=440 hertz (Hz).

TIPCODE

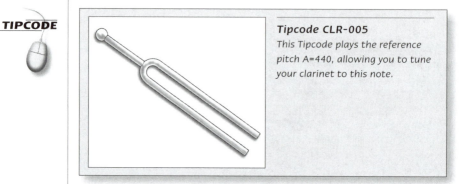

Tipcode CLR-005
This Tipcode plays the reference pitch A=440, allowing you to tune your clarinet to this note.

Sound little higher

Some ensembles tune a fraction higher, for instance to A=442. That ever-so-slight adjustment makes instruments sound just a little brighter or more brilliant.

Different tunings

Ideally, your clarinet must be built to the tuning of the orchestra. For this reason, most quality clarinets come in both 440Hz and 442Hz versions, and some even in a 444Hz tuning. For each tuning, the toneholes are distributed along the clarinet slightly differently. If you do occasionally need to make your instrument sound higher or lower, you can use a longer or shorter barrel (see page 95).

Tipcode CLR-006
The difference between A=440 and A=442 may not be that obvious at first. Playing the two pitches simultaneously clearly produces two 'beats' per second, caused by the 2Hz pitch difference.

THE MECHANISM

The mechanism should feel nice and smooth under your fingers, and it shouldn't rattle or produce other unwanted noises. A play-testing tip: If you operate the keywork without playing the instrument, it's easy to tell whether the keys and levers are quiet enough. Use all the keys, and pay special attention to the ones you operate with your left little finger.

A proper seal
The mechanism must ensure that all the keys close properly. If a key doesn't seal the tonehole, you won't be able to play that note — and possibly lots of others — properly, if at all. Usually this is a matter of adjustment, but a leaking key can also be caused by a torn pad, for instance.

Needle springs
Each key has a spring, which makes sure the key opens again after you've closed it, or the other way around. Some keys use *needle springs*. These springs do indeed look like needles.

Leaf springs
The trill keys, the A key, and the register key (the *see-saw* keys), have *leaf springs*, which are narrow metal strips. On a well-adjusted instrument, the springs are set to give all keys the same resistance.

55

Smooth

Keys should move smoothly. If their springs are adjusted too lightly, however, you may find that you can't really feel what you're doing, or that the keys become sluggish and don't return as quickly as they should. If a spring is much too lightly adjusted you may even blow the key open when you play the instrument really loudly.

Rings

If the rings are too high when open, it's hard to seal the toneholes with your fingers. If they are too low, the coupled keys won't respond immediately as they should. Some clarinetists like their ring keys to have a fairly high adjustment, others prefer them set quite low.

Proper fit

Some clarinets appear to be built for large hands, others for small hands, or for thick fingers or thin ones. You probably won't notice such differences fully until you take the time to play the instrument. The position and shape of the left little finger levers in particular can vary. A tip: Some companies make low-budget clarinets with mechanisms made especially for children's hands (see page 23).

The differences are often greatest at the left little finger levers. In particular, look at the (auxiliary) E♭ lever.

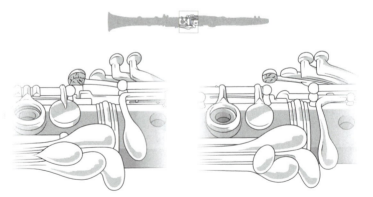

Adjustable thumb rest

An adjustable thumb rest can make the instrument more comfortable to play. Some clarinets have a coin-adjustable rest, which requires no extra tools. The illustration on the opposite page shows such a thumb rest (left), as well as an adjustable thumb rest with a strap ring, and a basic, fixed thumb rest (right).

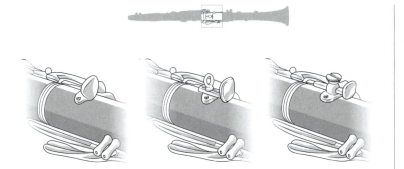

Three types of thumb rest.

Thumb saver

If the thumb rest cuts into your thumb, spend a few dollars on a rubber *thumb saver*. This small but useful accessory simply slides over the thumb rest.

Special thumb rests

When you play, the entire weight of the clarinet rests on the furthest joint of your thumb. This can cause pain and other symptoms, especially when you're playing for long stretches at a time. To avoid this, you may want to invest in a ergonomic thumb rests that divert the weight of the instrument to the first joint.

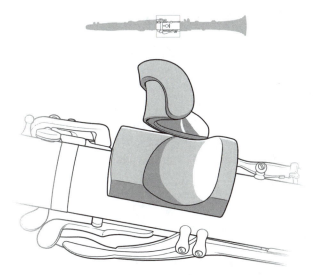

Ergonomic thumb rest (Kooiman).

57

Neckstrap

Another way to reduce the pressure on the thumb is to use a neckstrap (see page 22). Although typically used by children, these are increasingly popular with adult clarinetists.

Nickel or silver

Most low budget clarinets have nickel-plated mechanism, and the same goes for the entry-level instruments of some of the traditional clarinet makers. Silver-plated keywork is available as an option in some cases; other companies reserve silver plating for their slightly more expensive clarinets, with prices around seven of eight hundred dollars. A few companies also make five hundred dollar instruments with silver plating.

TIP

The differences

The difference between nickel and silver-plating is clearly visible: Nickel has a slightly 'harder' shine than silver, and silver looks a bit whiter. Nickel is less expensive, it needs less polishing, and is more resilient than silver. On the other hand, nickel feels more slippery, which can be a problem if you tend to have sweaty fingers. If you suffer from a nickel allergy, you will need to buy an instrument with silver-plated keywork, of course.

Gold

If you have very acidic perspiration, it can make silver tarnish so quickly that you're better off with a nickel-plated mechanism. As an alternative, you can have your keywork gold-plated, which is less expensive than it sounds. New clarinets with a fully or partly gold-plated mechanism are rare, but they are available.

Posts

On some models only the *posts* are gold-plated. The posts are the small pillars that attach the keywork to the clarinet. Often, some of the posts are anchored to the instrument by a small screw which resists the pressure of the needle spring that could otherwise rotate the post.

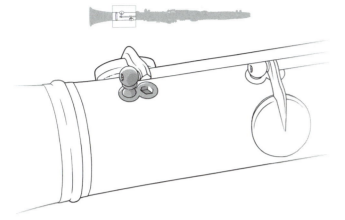

An anchored
post.

Black

For a completely different look, some companies offer clarinets
with a black-anodized keywork.

> ### Nickel-silver
>
> *The keywork itself is usually made of nickel-silver. That
> sounds more expensive than it is: Nickel-silver is an alloy of
> copper, nickel and zinc. The only link with silver is the general
> appearance of the material. Even the exact mixture of these
> ingredients and other factors that influence the relative
> hardness of the keywork can play a role in the sound of your
> instrument. A 'harder' keywork typically contributes to a
> brighter, 'harder' sound.*

Rounded or pointed keys

Virtually all clarinets have so-called *French-style keys*, indicating
that the key cups are attached to a pointed arm. The key cups
come in two varieties: *rounded* (also called *rond-bombé*) or in a
slightly *pointed shape* (*conical* or *China cup*).

Power-forged keys

Most clarinets have *power-forged* keys, meaning that they are
shaped by pressure, when the metal is cold, rather than cast.

59

Trill keys

The trill keys come in two types. *Offset trill keys* have a kink just before the key cup; *in-line trill keys* don't. The movement of the key cups is a little more logical with the in-line system, as it moves vertically up and down, rather than slightly diagonally. The difference isn't very meaningful, though, and you find both systems on both low-budget and professional instruments.

Offset (above) and in-line trill keys.

Separate mountings

What does make a difference is whether certain keys are individually mounted, having separate post mountings. If so, they tend to be easier to adjust, and the keywork may last longer. On most more expensive clarinets, each trill key is individually mounted, while on less expensive instruments the B♭ and B-keys share their posts. Some lower budget clarinets also have only three posts by the A and A♭ keys, instead of four. More expensive clarinets may have more individually mounted keys, e.g., the C♯/ G♯ and the A♭/E♭ keys.

Adjustment screws

Pretty much all clarinets have an adjustment screw on the A and A♭ keys, on the upper part of the left-hand joint. You'll find other adjustment screws only on more expensive clarinets. Typically,

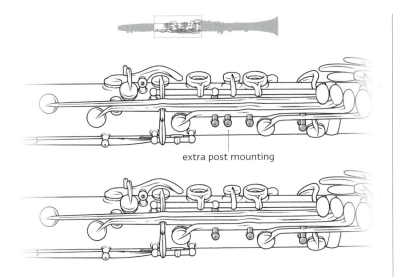

extra post mounting

An individually-mounted A♭/E♭ key (above), and a regular one.

the F♯/C♯ and E/B keys will be adjustable, with two extra screws under the *crow foot* by your right little finger. Very occasionally, the F/C key will also have an adjustment screw, or the bridge will. Of course, a clarinet can also be adjusted without screws, but only with some very careful bending. The mechanism of very low-budget clarinets is often harder to adjust or repair. Some clarinet technicians won't even work on such instruments.

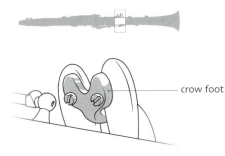

— crow foot

Adjustment screws, hidden under the crow foot.

Cork

Various keys need to be adjusted by sticking pieces of cork of varying thickness under them. This is a job that you'd better leave to a specialist. Corks are also used to make the mechanism quieter, by keeping parts from clattering against each other.

TIP

> ## Large clarinets and German clarinets
>
> Bass and alto clarinets and other larger instruments, with much longer key rods, usually have more adjustment screws. Clarinets with German mechanisms often have a whole bunch too.

EXTRA KEYS

The majority of French or Boehm clarinets have a standard mechanism, featuring seventeen keys and six rings (17/6). Other models provide you with extra keys and other features.

Auxiliary E♭ lever

Quite a few clarinets in the higher price ranges have four levers by the left little finger, instead of the usual three. If so, you're dealing with an 18/6 clarinet. The extra fourth lever is known as the *auxiliary E♭(/A♭) lever,* doubling the right-hand little finger lever for that key. Some series offer this addition as an option that typically costs you some hundred to two hundred dollars.

Forked B♭

A seventh ring key allows you to play a B♭ by using your left ring finger and index finger. This *forked fingering* is called a *forked B♭* or *fork B♭.* The seventh ring also makes certain trills easier.

Articulated G♯

Even rarer than the fork B♭ is the *articulated G♯* or *F♯/ G♯ trill key,* found on 19/7 clarinets. An articulated G♯ can be identified

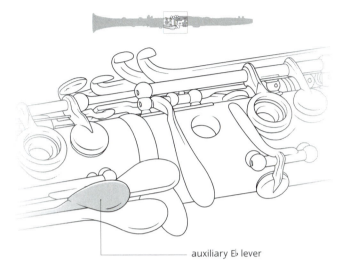

auxiliary E♭ lever

The auxiliary E♭ lever is the fourth lever by the left little finger.

by the extra closed-hole key under the G♯ lever. Also, there is an extra lever on the lower joint. The key allows you to play various trills with your right hand index finger without using your left-hand little finger.

Low E♭

A clarinet with a low E♭ is just a little longer than a regular B♭ soprano. You play the extra low note on such a 20/7 clarinet with a fifth key by your right little finger.

Full Boehm

A clarinet with all the above extras is known as a *full Boehm* instrument. Only very few manufacturers still make them. How come? Because all the additions make for a heavier instrument with a less bright tone, because an articulated G♯ is a complicated affair, and because the seventh ring makes some trills easier but others impossible. As a result, the standard 17/6 remains the most popular instrument, and there's hardly anything you can't play on it.

Low E vent key

Other options are available too. For example, the occasional clarinet has a so-called *low E vent key*. If you play a low E or F, a key opens an extra tonehole at the end of the lower joint, or in

63

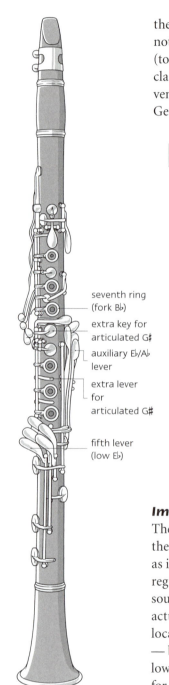

A full-Boehm
clarinet.

seventh ring
(fork B♭)

extra key for
articulated G♯

auxiliary E♭/A♭
lever

extra lever
for
articulated G♯

fifth lever
(low E♭)

the bell. This slightly raises those two
notes, which often sound a little *flat*
(too low), especially so on German
clarinets. This explains why low E
vent keys are much more common on
German instruments.

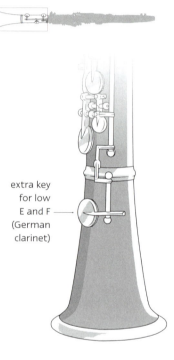

extra key
for low
E and F
(German
clarinet)

Improved B♭

The B♭ of the chalumeau register is
the hardest note for clarinet makers,
as it uses the same tonehole as the
register key. In order to make that B♭
sound really good, the tonehole would
actually need to be a bit bigger and
located a bit lower on the instrument
— but then it would be too big and too
low to function as an effective tonehole
for the register key.

64

Extra key

German system clarinets often have an extra key to make the
B♭ sound a little clearer. Many solutions have been provided to
improve its pitch on French clarinets too, such as a pitch adjustable
aftermarket replacement for the A-tonehole.

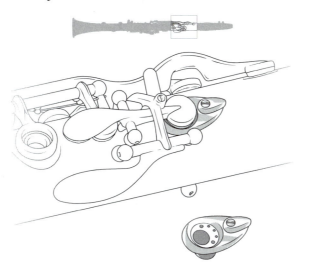

Adjustable aftermarket tonehole to improve B♭ (Tutz).

Bass clarinet to low C

Bass clarinets always have a low E♭, and many go down to a low C.
How you play those lowest notes varies per brand, and sometimes
even per model. On some instruments, you operate three keys
with your right thumb and five with your little finger; on others
you'll play two with your thumb and six with your little finger, for
example.

> #### Differences
> The larger range low-C bass clarinet can easily cost a
> thousand dollars more than an identical instrument with E♭
> as its lowest note. Some players prefer the smaller E♭ models
> simply because they find them easier to handle.

Second register key

In order to improve response and intonation, some larger clarinets

65

have two register keys. Which of the two keys opens depends on the note you are playing. For some notes in the highest register, bass clarinets also have a small extra hole in the key cup under your left index finger: To play those notes you close the key, leaving the extra hole open.

PADS

To ensure that the keys seal the toneholes properly, they are fitted with pads. Usually a pad consists of a layer of felt covered with a very thin, vulnerable membrane. This membrane is often referred to as *fish skin*, but it actually comes from cows' intestines. Most pads have two or even three layers.

Plastic
Synthetic pads are becoming more and more common on clarinets. They are not affected by moisture or dryness as much as traditional pads, they last longer, but they're more expensive.

Cork
The keys at the bottom of the tube may have cork pads, because they are the most likely to become waterlogged by the moisture that collects in the instrument. Some players prefer cork pads for the other keys, making the sound a little brighter. Bass clarinets often have cork pads on the register key and other, smaller keys.

Leather
The other pads of most larger clarinets are made of very thin goat (kid) leather. German clarinets often have leather pads as well, to make for a slightly darker timbre than 'fish skin' pads do. These leather pads, too, are increasingly being replaced by synthetic pads.

Resonators
Some clarinets have metal *resonators* in the pads of the last keys of the lower joint; these slightly enhance brightness and projection.

> ### Kangaroo
>
> *A growing number of clarinet makers and technicians use kangaroo leather pads. Kangaroo leather is very strong and lightweight, and it is claimed that kangaroo leather pads don't stick, produce less noise, and last much longer than regular (goat) leather pads.*

THE A CLARINET

Clarinetists in a symphony orchestra will almost always have two clarinets: a B♭ clarinet and a slightly longer A clarinet, which sounds a half step lower. An A clarinet also has a slightly different timbre, and is a lot easier to play in certain keys. For instance, a piece in A major concert pitch has five sharps for a B♭ clarinet, and none at all for an A clarinet. If you're playing the latter instrument, you simply play this piece in C major.

Differences

The A clarinet is said to sound a little sweeter, darker, milder, mellower, or richer than a B♭ clarinet. Some clarinetists think the difference is quite marked, others say you only really hear it well at the bottom end of the highest register. Similarly, many composers insist that an A clarinet or a B♭ clarinet be used for specific compositions, while others tend to leave it to the clarinetist.

GERMAN CLARINETS

In Germany and Austria, most clarinetists play 'German clarinets'. These instruments have a slightly different sound, and also a different mechanism. This mechanism comes in many different variations. Albert, Oehler, and reform Boehm are the three best known systems.

67

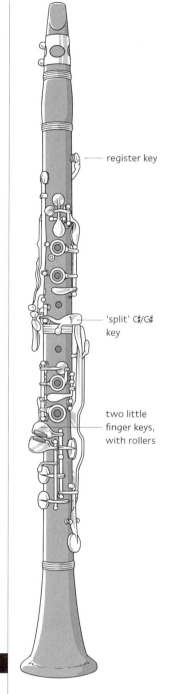

A German clarinet with the Albert system.

register key

'split' C♯/G♯ key

two little finger keys, with rollers

Sound

German clarinets sound different from French ones. How different? Most experts say that German clarinets sound darker, more robust, thicker, fuller, or sweeter, with the French (Boehm) sound being described as brighter, lighter, more open, and more delicate. Others will tell you the opposite, though.

Different bore

The difference in sound between German and French (Boehm) clarinets lies largely in the bore. One main difference is that German clarinets begin to flare out beyond only the E/B key, rather than halfway down the lower joint. In other words, the cylindrical section of the bore is much longer than on a French instrument. The mouthpiece and reed are different too, as you can read in the chapters that follow.

Larger or smaller?

Many clarinetists think that the bore of German clarinets is larger than that of French clarinets; others will tell you that it is smaller. The truth is that bores vary from brand to brand. Some German clarinet makers use a small bore diameter of around 0.575" (14.6 mm), which is slightly smaller than most French ones. Others prefer a large bore of 0.590" (15 mm), being as wide as the largest French bore. So it's not the exact diameter of the bore at a certain point that makes the

68

difference, but the shape of the entire bore, from the top to the bottom of the instrument!

Little finger keys

The easiest way to tell you're looking at a German clarinet is by the right little finger keys. There are only two of them, with a roller to help you move from key to key. The left little finger keys are different from the ones on a French clarinet too.

Split design key, curved lever

If you look carefully you'll notice other differences too: For instance, the C♯/G♯ key has a 'split' design, which allows you to operate it with your right little finger as well. The lever of the register key has been curved, as the hole that it covers is located at the front side of the instrument, rather than of at the back.

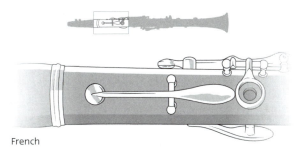

French

German

On German clarinets, the register key lever has been moved nearer the front of the tube.

Albert system

German clarinets come with various different mechanisms. In Germany and Austria, students usually start out on an instrument with the Albert system, which has nineteen or twenty keys, and between four, five, or six ring keys.

TIP

Oehler system

Most advanced and professional German clarinetists play instruments with the *Oehler system*. You can recognize an Oehler clarinet by the one plateau key by the right middle finger, and by the two F-resonance keys on the lower joint. Those two extra keys make the F and the low B♭ brighter, and better in tune.

The Oehler system is easy to recognize by the plateau-style key by the right middle finger and the two F-resonance keys on the side.

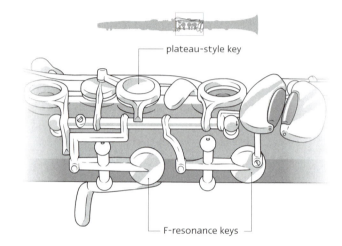

plateau-style key

F-resonance keys

Full Oehler

Oehler clarinets come in all kinds of variations. The simplest version has twenty-one keys, and so-called *full Oehlers* may have as many as twenty-seven.

Why French?

The French system is favored in most countries around the world because it is easier to play than the German one. For example, you need fewer forked fingerings, and there are more notes you can play in different ways.

German with French

The *reform Boehm* or *German Boehm* clarinet allows you to play with a French mechanism but still sound German. This type of clarinet has a German bore, and hence a German sound, but a French (Boehm) mechanism. The keywork can be slightly different on a few points; for instance, it may have a double F/C key, or rollers between the right little finger keys.

Even more systems

There are many other, lesser known systems as well, such as the Schmidt-Kolbe system, with lots of additional keys, or the old Müller system. Clarinets with these systems are hardly found outside central Europe. In Austria, clarinet players use *Austrian clarinets*, with a large bore and a mechanism that varies slightly from the Oehler keywork.

German system

In Germany, the Albert system is known as the *German system*, the other two being referred to with their specific names (i.e., Oehler and reform Boehm). The name Albert is only really used outside Germany.

IN TUNE

In order to really play a clarinet in tune, you need to correct certain notes even on the best instrument. The better the clarinet, the more inherently in tune it will be, and the less correcting you need to do. In other words, the better a clarinet's intonation, the easier it will be to play in tune.

Out of tune

To judge a clarinet's intonation you need to be able to play pretty well. If not, you'll never know whether it's the clarinet or you that is out of tune.

Too small, too big

A clarinet could only be made completely in tune if it had three

---

Tuning ratios

The exact placement of the tonehole of the register key influences the tuning ratios of the instrument, i.e., the pitch differences between E/B, F/C, and so on.

TIP

71

or more register keys, and that would make the mechanism much too complicated. So there's only one, and that one register key can never be in the right position for all tone combinations (E/B, F/C, and so on).

Always different

It's not just the register key tonehole that determines the intonation of a clarinet. Other factors include the positions and shapes of the toneholes, the bore, the barrel, and the mouthpiece. Every manufacturer chooses its own solutions to make the intonation of its clarinets as good as possible. So which notes you have to correct and by how much can vary from one brand to another, and even from one model to another.

All the same

This is one reason why many groups and orchestras prefer all their clarinetists to play the same type of clarinet, aiming to make the clarinet section sound as a whole.

All different

Every clarinet is different. Take that into account when you are play-testing clarinets. If you are used to a clarinet on which a certain note always tends to sound flat, that note may suddenly seem sharp (too high) on a 'better' clarinet because you are compensating too much for it. That can make a good clarinet sound as if it has bad intonation.

TIP

Too short, too low

Sometimes, certain notes may be sharp or flat by such an amount that you'll never get them in tune. This may be caused by, for example, using a mouthpiece that doesn't match the instrument, or a barrel that's too long or too short, or by certain keys that open too far, or not far enough. A key that doesn't open far enough can make certain notes sound flat and stuffy. If the key opening or venting is too big, some notes will be sharp.

Only a few

There are only a few notes that are either sharp (e.g., B4 and C5) or flat (e.g., E3, F3, F2) on just about every clarinet. There are also some notes that are sharp on most clarinets, but flat on others. This is particularly true of the notes you play with most of the keys open, i.e., the highest four notes of the chalumeau register (G4 and up). These are called the *short-pipe* or *short-tube notes*, because you only use a 'short' section of the clarinet to play them.

AUDITIONING CLARINETS

Your favorite clarinet has a beautiful tone, of course — but what beautiful is strongly depends on your taste and the type of music you play. A clarinet should also have an even timbre and tuning, whether you play soft or loud, high or low, and long-tube or short-tube notes.

Another player

In order to choose a clarinet by its sound, you need to be able to play at least reasonably well. If you can't play yet or haven't been playing very long, take a good clarinetist with you to try out testing tips, or go to a store that employs one.

Somebody else

If you get somebody else to play a bunch of clarinets for you, they'll never sound the same as if you were to play them yourself — but you will be able to hear the differences between the instruments. A tip: Even if you do play yourself, ask somebody else to play for you, just to hear how the various clarinets sound from a distance. You'll find that you hear things you didn't hear before. If there's no other clarinetist available, you can point the instruments at a wall so that their sound is reflected back to you.

Same barrel, same mouthpiece

Only if you play every clarinet with the same mouthpiece and barrel will you hear the differences between clarinets, rather than

73

the differences between mouthpieces and barrels. Preferably use your own mouthpiece and barrel to start with, but be aware that some clarinets will perform better with a different combination.

... with the same mouthpiece and barrel ...

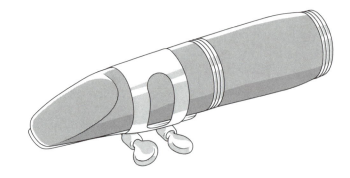

Briefly at first

If you have a whole selection of clarinets in front of you, choosing is often easiest if you only play each instrument briefly. Play something simple, otherwise you'll be concentrating more on playing than on listening. Scales, for instance, nice and slowly. A tip: It may be that you prefer the sound of one clarinet to all the others straight away. That'll often be the clarinet you end up buying.

Two by two

Once you've found a number of clarinets that you really like, compare them two by two or three by three. Choose the best one and replace the one you like least with another clarinet. Again choose the best one, and so on.

For your ears only

Try listening to the same clarinets without looking to see which one you're playing. This allows you to choose with your ears only, without being influenced by the price, the brand name or anything else. If the clarinet that sounds best and plays best turns out to be the least expensive one, that's a bonus. Unless you particularly wanted a more expensive one, of course.

74

A little longer

In order to select the very best clarinet from the two or three that remain, you may want to play each instrument a little longer so that you get to know it better.

A tip: Even after just fifteen minutes of playing it gets harder to hear the differences between clarinets. Take a break, or come back a day or two later.

Sheet music

If you don't know any music by heart, take a few pieces with you when you go to choose a clarinet. The better you know a piece, the less you will be thinking about the notes, and the better you can listen to the instrument that you're playing.

Where to start

If you have no idea where to start when you walk into a store, ask for two clarinets with very different timbres or characters. One with a notably dark tone and another that sounds particularly bright, for example, or one with a small bore and one with a large bore. Decide what you like best and go on from there. Or try a very affordable clarinet alongside the most expensive one in the store, simply to hear how much difference it makes.

Your own clarinet

Take your own clarinet with you to the store, if you have one. That makes it easier to hear just how different instruments sound. On the other hand: You may be so used to your own instrument that it may seem to sound better or more in tune than other clarinets — even much more expensive and better ones.

WHAT TO LISTEN FOR

Comparing sounds is something you have to learn how to do; the more often you do it, the more you hear. It also helps if you know what kind of things you can listen for, which is explained on the following pages.

75

What you like

When two people listen to the same clarinet they often use very different words to describe what they hear. What one considers shrill and thin (and so not attractive), another may consider bright or brilliant (and so not unattractive). And what one describes as warm, dark or velvety, another may think dim, dull or stuffy. It all depends on what you like, on how you perceive sound, and on the words you use to describe it.

Character

What sounds good and what doesn't also depends on the kind of music you play. If you play classical music, you're probably looking for a darker, warmer sound than if you play jazz or folk music. Some clarinets allow you to play different styles easier than others, being less versatile.

Easy

Some clarinets blow more easily than others. That's mainly to do with the bore. A clarinet with little blowing resistance plays easily and usually has a big, open tone. Classical players generally prefer an instrument with more resistance and a darker sound. If a clarinet has too much resistance, the sound will become dull, stuffy or lifeless.

Resistance

When you play long-tube notes you will of course feel a bit more resistance or pressure than when you play short-tube ones. That difference is bigger with some clarinets than others. The smaller the difference, the easier it is to make the instrument sound even, whether you're playing high, low, short-tube, or long-tube notes. In other words, right-hand notes should not have much more resistance than left-hand notes.

High and low

The high notes sound different from the low ones on all clarinets, but the better the instrument, the smaller the difference will be. The low notes should sound firm, deep, and clear, even when you're playing softly. The high notes must not sound shrill, edgy, or metallic, even when you're playing loudly.

Loud and soft

To test a clarinet, go from high to low playing loudly, and then do the same playing softly. Notice whether the instrument responds equally, whether you make each note sound separately or join all the notes together (legato).

Rising and falling

When you go from loud to soft, and the other way around, check that the pitch doesn't change too much. On clarinets, the pitch has a tendency to fall as you get louder, and to rise when you get softer. Funny: With most other instruments it's the other way around.

Problem notes

When you are comparing the sounds of different clarinets, pay special attention to the notes G4 to Bb4, i.e., the highest notes of the chalumeau register. Those are the clarinet's traditional 'problem notes'. The Bb4 is particularly tricky. If that note sounds really good, you're likely to have a great clarinet in your hands. This group of tricky short-tube notes is known as the *throat register* or the *break register*.

Tipcode CLR-007
Here are the clarinet's problem notes, G4 to Bb4.

TIPCODE

PRE-OWNED INSTRUMENTS

When you go to buy a pre-owned clarinet, there are a few extra things you should remember. To begin with, always put the clarinet together yourself, so you can check that the fit between the sections isn't too tight or too loose. They should fit together so snugly that the clarinet feels as though it was made from a single piece of wood.

Leaks

Check that all notes respond well. If not, there's a fair chance that air is leaking somewhere. That could be due to a torn pad, a poorly adjusted ring or key, or a leak between two joints. Air can also escape from around the register tube.

Check

To check the clarinet joints for leaks, first take the upper joint, close all the toneholes, and block one end with your hand. Then put your lips around the other end, and suck. If you inhale any air, there is a leak somewhere. Do the same with the lower joint.

Springs

When you've checked the lower joint this way, again block one end, and blow. If that makes the C♯ and E♭ keys open up, their springs should be adjusted to provide a little more resistance.

Play

Check carefully whether keys and levers can only move up and down, not sideways or back and forth. Older instruments often

Check these and other keys for play.

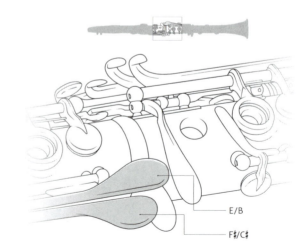

E/B

F♯/C♯

suffer from play on the F♯/C♯ and the E/B by the left little finger, caused by excessive wear of the linkage components. This makes playing uncomfortable, it may cause leaks and noise, and it always gets worse in time.

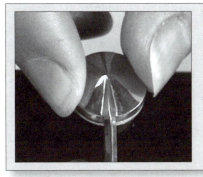

Tipcode CLR-008
The levers and keys of your instrument should be — carefully — checked for play, from time to time. A brief demonstration is shown in this Tipcode.

TIPCODE

Noise

Noise and buzzing sounds may also be due to poor adjustment, a missing cork, torn pads, loose or missing springs, or a loose metal bell ring, tenon ring, or body ring. If a ring is loose, it may be that the clarinet has been stored in a room with very low air humidity, which increases the chances that the wood will crack — now or later.

Cracks

Wooden clarinets always need to be checked for cracks. The most likely places to find cracks are the tenons, and the toneholes by the A, A♭, and trill keys. Small cracks can often be effectively repaired.

The bore

Look down through the bore, and do the same with the barrel and the mouthpiece. If the previous owner took good care of the instrument, everything will look smooth on the inside and it will smell only of clarinet.

Mouthpiece

Also inspect the outside of the mouthpiece. If there are teeth marks in it, your own teeth will naturally be forced into the same position. Pay special attention to the edges or *rails* (see page 89):

79

Even minor damage in those areas can render a mouthpiece unusable. In the following chapter you will read why even a good mouthpiece with slight damage may be no use to you.

Appraisal

It's always a good idea to have a used clarinet appraised by an expert. Then you'll know what it's worth, and what it may cost you to have it adjusted or repaired. To give you an idea: A crack can often be repaired for around fifty dollars, and for some four to five hundred dollars or more you may get an old, worn-out clarinet made as good as new.

6

Mouthpieces, Ligatures, and Barrels

The sound of a clarinet depends on who is playing it, more than anything else. Almost as important is the reed, followed by the mouthpiece and the barrel — and even the ligature contributes to the end result.

Some mouthpieces are easier to play than others. If you are just starting out, it's nice to have one that plays easily — though a mouthpiece like that usually won't get you the dark tone that many clarinetists are after. If you've been playing a little longer, the best mouthpiece is one that allows you to play loudly and softly, high and low, and staccato and legato with equal ease and a balanced, stable timbre and pitch.

The clarinet
You can't simply put any mouthpiece on any clarinet. A poorly chosen mouthpiece will physically 'fit,' but it can make the instrument sound out of tune, edgy, dull, or unbalanced.

You
A mouthpiece also has to suit you. That includes your embouchure, your technique, and the sound you are looking for.

Almost everybody
Then there are mouthpieces that almost everybody feels comfortable with. Such mouthpieces are often used in orchestras or groups in which all clarinetists play the same brand of instrument.

A good replacement
Such 'user-friendly' mouthpieces also make a good first replacement for the low-budget mouthpieces that come with most student clarinets. The latter often make for an edgy or harsh sound, and they're often quite hard to play. This can make half an hour's practice seem like a very long time.

Keep looking
Also, using one of these user-friendly mouthpieces will probably give you a good starting point if you later decide to try out some more different ones. And you can be sure that there's enough to choose from, right up to hand-made or even customized mouthpieces. The least expensive mouthpiece models typically set you back some twenty to thirty dollars. Professional mouthpieces start around seventy-five to a hundred dollars, going up to three hundred dollars or even more.

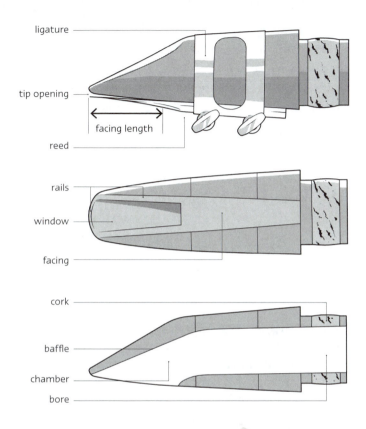

A mouthpiece shown from the side, from below and in cross-section.

In brief

When you go out to buy a mouthpiece, you're bound to come across the following terms:

- The *tip opening* is the space between the tip of the reed and the tip of the mouthpiece.

- The *facing length* is the distance from the tip opening to where the reed first touches the mouthpiece. It's not just the length of the facing (or *lay*) that matters, but also its curvature.

- The opening that is closed off by the reed is called the *window* or *wind cut*.

- Behind the window is the *chamber*.

- The other end, where the mouthpiece connects with the barrel, is the *bore*.

83

Dimensions or words?

On their websites and in their brochures, mouthpiece makers usually state the exact sizes of the tip opening and facing length of each of their mouthpieces. On their own, these figures don't tell you too much: A mouthpiece has many more dimensions that affect its performance. So it's usually more useful to read what the mouthpiece maker says about the sound you can expect from a certain mouthpiece, and about the style of music for which it has been designed. A very subdued sound, for instance, for chamber music. Or a sound that blends well, for symphonic work. Lots of volume and projection, for orchestras that play outdoors, or great flexibility, for jazz.

Different brand, different sound

Each mouthpiece brand tends to have its own 'character'. The mouthpieces of Brand A may sound very direct, bright or edgy, the products of Brand B may have a little warmer sound, while those of Brand C offer more resistance and a darker timbre. Which brands fit those descriptions usually depends on who you ask, though.

Easy

Some clarinetists spend their whole lives looking for the ideal mouthpiece. Others are much less demanding, or they have an 'easy embouchure': It doesn't matter much which mouthpiece they use, and reeds pretty much always work fine for them as well.

One or more

Similarly, there are clarinetists who use one and the same mouthpiece for all kinds of different musical styles, and others who use two, three or more different mouthpieces, each with its own character.

Knitted cord

German clarinets have very different mouthpieces to French ones, with smaller tip openings and longer facings. The reed is

usually not attached with a ligature but with a knitted cord . Some
'French' players use that method too. The Tipcode below shows
you how that works.

Tipcode CLR-009
German clarinetists often use a
cord rather than a ligature. Here's
how they do it.

TIPCODE

German on French
If you fit a German mouthpiece on a French clarinet, you'll
immediately hear how much influence the mouthpiece has on the
sound: It makes a French clarinet sound very 'German.' While
some experts tend to disapprove of doing so, other clarinetists
always use this particular combination. Note that this may require
a slight modification of the mouthpiece or the barrel.

Mouthpiece tips
If you are going out to choose a new mouthpiece, the following
tips may be of use:

• Make sure you know roughly **what you are looking for**. A
good salesperson will then be able to recommend a handful of
mouthpieces, so that you won't have to try dozens.

• Take your **own clarinet and mouthpiece** with you for
comparison.

• If you always use a **mouthpiece cushion** (see pages 92–93), don't
test other mouthpieces without one. A mouthpiece cushion also
prevents you leaving tooth marks in new mouthpieces.

• Don't compare twenty different mouthpieces at once. Instead,
choose three, listen, and replace the one you like least with
another. And so on.

85

- **Take breaks**: After a quarter of an hour of testing you won't be able to hear what you're doing nearly as well.

- Choosing the perfect mouthpiece quickly will always be difficult: You only really get to know a new mouthpiece **after a few weeks' playing**.

- Also, a mouthpiece won't perform to its full potential until you have found the right reed to go with it. A good salesperson can advise you on **good reed/mouthpiece combinations**.

- When you are testing mouthpieces, be sure to always use a **good, new reed**.

- When it comes to mouthpieces, **thousandths of an inch** can make a difference. That's why no two mouthpieces are exactly the same. Even if you know exactly which mouthpiece you want, it's still worth trying out a few of the same type: There's a good chance you'll like one better than another.

THE DIFFERENCES

How a mouthpiece plays and sounds depends on the tip opening, the length and curvature of the facing, the material, and much else besides.

Names and numbers

Almost all manufacturers use combinations of letters and numbers to identify their different mouthpieces. Sadly, those 'codes' usually tell you nothing. For instance, with one brand a higher number means a larger tip opening, with another it means a smaller one.

Similar mouthpiece, different code

As an example, the Vandoren B45, the Leblanc L4, and the Selmer 120 are three comparable mouthpieces — but you wouldn't think so if you only looked at their codes. There are only a few brands that print the dimensions of the tip, the facing and the chamber on their mouthpieces.

Tables

To make your quest a bit easier, there are tables listing the characteristics of mouthpieces by different brands side by side. You may find these tables online as well as in music stores.

The whole thing

Everything to do with mouthpieces is interrelated. For instance, two mouthpieces with the same tip opening and the same facing length may nevertheless sound and play very differently. Or one of them may work brilliantly on one clarinet and terribly on another. In the end, it's a matter of trying them out until you find the perfect combination, in which clarinet, mouthpiece, reed, barrel, and ligature together sound and play exactly the way you want them to.

TIP OPENING

Tip openings of clarinet mouthpieces are usually stated in thousandths of an inch. Most clarinet mouthpieces have a tip opening between 0.040" and 0.050" (roughly 1–1.3 mm).

Reed size

For beginners, the best choice often is a soft to medium-soft reed, such as a 1.5 or a 2, on a mouthpiece with a tip opening of around 0.045–0.047" (roughly 1.15– 1.19 mm). This tip opening is not too big (which helps avoid pitch fluctuations), and not too small (because you'd need too much air). A versatile mouthpiece that suits clarinetists in all kinds of different styles is likely to have a similar, medium-sized tip opening.

Small

A smaller tip opening usually means a darker sound and more resistance. A small opening also requires a harder reed: If the reed were too soft, it would vibrate over too great a distance. Since a harder reed doesn't move up and down as far, pitch and sound are not as easy to adjust. If the tip opening is too small, the result may be a dull, stuffy tone, a sharp pitch, and an exhausted player.

87

Large

A large tip opening makes playing easier, it opens up the sound, and you get more volume and a more vivid tone. There's a lot of scope for correcting tone and pitch, allowing you to slide from note to note, for instance. The fact that you *can* correct more also means you always *have to* correct more. A large tip requires a relatively soft reed that allows for relatively large movements. The largest tip opening is just under 0.060" (1.5 mm), but such mouthpieces are rare.

TIP

> ## Millimeters to inches
>
> *American brands usually give tip openings in thousandths of an inch. If you want to convert a 'European' tip opening, given in hundredths of a millimeter, to inches, divide by 25.4. An example: A tip opening 127 is actually 1.27 mm, and 1.27 ÷ 25.4 = 0.050". The other way around: an American size 50 would be 50 x 0.0254 = 1.27 mm.*

Other clarinets

Mouthpieces for larger and smaller clarinets naturally have larger and smaller tip openings, respectively. The tip opening of a bass clarinet mouthpiece, for example, is usually somewhere between 0.060" and 0.080" (1.5–2mm), while E♭ clarinet mouthpieces start under 0.430" (1.1 mm).

THE FACING

On its own, the facing length doesn't tell you very much. It's the combination of the facing length and the tip opening that's really important. An example: A small tip opening with a long facing gives a good response, with a dark, rich tone. But if you combine that same facing length with a large tip opening, you will get a brighter tone and more volume.

Curvature and facing

At least as important is the curvature of the facing, though most mouthpiece makers tell you next to nothing about that. The main reason is that it is not easy to describe how 'curved' a facing is.

All-purpose facing

The term *facing* is also used to indicate the length and the curvature of the lay, as well as the tip opening, which are closely related of course. A mouthpiece with an *all-purpose facing* has a medium-sized tip opening and a medium-length facing that is neither too curved nor too flat.

Long or short

On French mouthpieces, the facing length typically varies between about 0.710" and 0.865" (18–22 mm). A longer facing allows for a broader, bigger sound; a shorter facing is more likely to produce a more focused, centered sound.

Words or letters

The facing length is often indicated using words or letters rather than figures. A tip: What one brand calls short, another brand may call medium.

The rails

The edges or *rails* of the mouthpiece are also part of the facing. If the *side rails* are not exactly the same shape and thickness, the mouthpiece will be out of balance. As a result, you may get squeaks, or your instrument may have a poor response or a shrill sound.

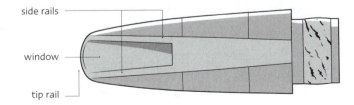

side rails

window

tip rail

89

Sound

The thickness of the side rails and the *tip rail* also affect the tone. Thicker rails make the sound thicker and darker, while narrower edges give a brighter sound. If the rails are too thick, the sound becomes dull. If they are too narrow, the instrument will sound harsh or edgy.

Wear

Most mouthpieces are made of hard rubber. This material is less hard than it appears, and hard rubber mouthpieces actually wear out in time, due to cleaning, your teeth, and the fact that the reed constantly beats the mouthpiece when you play: A clarinet has what is officially known as a *beating reed*. If you're finding it very hard to find a reed that works with your instrument, or if your tone is growing shrill and harsh, try a new mouthpiece. You may find out your old one has worn out.

CHAMBER, BAFFLE, BORE, AND TABLE

A mouthpiece with a large chamber typically has a dark, warm, full sound that is especially well suited to classical music. For a bright, vivid sound with a good projection, you're usually better off with a mouthpiece that has a smaller chamber.

Baffle

Some mouthpieces have a *baffle*, as shown in the illustration on page 83. This lowering of the chamber's 'ceiling' (the *palate*) compresses the air, making the sound brighter and increasing the projection. Conversely, a concave palate would make the sound darker.

Bore

There are special mouthpieces for instruments with large or small bores, but you don't usually need to pay special attention to the bore of the mouthpiece itself. If you are interested, though, the effect of the mouthpiece bore is comparable to that of the bore of the instrument: A small bore promotes a tighter, more focused, and darker sound, while a large bore contributes to a 'wider,' more open sound.

Table

The table, upon which the reed rests, is usually flat. On some mouthpieces, it is a tiny bit concave when looked at lengthwise. This slight depression is supposed to allow the reed to vibrate more freely, which in turn enables you to influence the sound a little more, whether by the tension of your lips or by your choice of ligature (see pages 98–100).

Beaks and bites

Mouthpieces differ in many other ways. The *beak angle* may vary, for instance. That means that the part you set your teeth on is either steeper or less steep than normal, making the mouthpiece feel either fatter or thinner. There are also mouthpieces that have been specially adapted for clarinetists with overbite or underbite.

MATERIALS

Most clarinetists use hard rubber (ebonite) mouthpieces. Alternatively, you can get mouthpieces made of plastic, crystal, metal, wood or other materials.

Ebonite

Ebonite mouthpieces tend to offer a fairly warm, dark sound, but there are some that can make your sound edgy and bright. This difference is due partly to the exact hardness of the material, but mostly to the shape of the mouthpiece.

Plastic

Plastic is mainly, but not exclusively, used for student mouthpieces. The sound is often quite hard and bright.

Crystal, glass, and metal

Most crystal mouthpieces are designed to generate a dark, warm sound, but some actually sound quite bright: Again, the dimensions of the mouthpiece are more influential than the material used. Crystal is very fragile, of course. Glass and metal mouthpieces are very rare.

Wood

Most wooden mouthpieces make clarinets sound extra dark and round. Because no two pieces of wood are the same, there can be big variations between two 'identical' mouthpieces. Wooden mouthpieces also react quickly to changes in temperature and air humidity.

MOUTHPIECE CUSHIONS

Most clarinetists use mouthpiece cushions or patches on their mouthpieces. These patches protect the mouthpiece from your teeth, and your teeth from the vibrations of the mouthpiece, providing a more comfortable feel. The material also gives you a bit of extra grip on the mouthpiece.

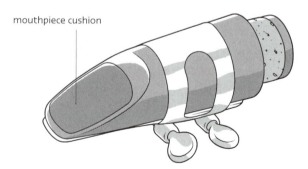

mouthpiece cushion

Thickness

Mouthpiece patches come in various thicknesses, e.g., 0.3 mm, 0.4 mm, 0.8 mm en 0.9 mm (0.012–0.035"). What works best for you is basically a matter of trial and error. Patches come at low prices, so that won't be a major problem.

Thick or thin

Thick patches offer more protection and playing comfort, but they may induce biting in the mouthpiece, for example, and they can make you open up your mouth slightly too widely.

Black, clear

Mouthpiece patches come in different colors, typically black and clear, the color basically being the only difference. Smaller patches are meant for smaller (e.g., B♭ clarinet) mouthpieces, and the larger models for larger (e.g., bass clarinet) mouthpieces.

Two more tips

- **Clean and dry** the outside your mouthpiece thoroughly before sticking a patch onto it.

- Use an extra thin patch to prevent **your ligature** from scratching your mouthpiece.

GERMAN MOUTHPIECES

German mouthpieces have a much smaller tip opening (approximately 0.025–0.040" or 0.65–1 mm) than French ones, and a longer facing (from around 0.730"– 0.985" or 18.5–25 mm, or more).

Window and walls

German mouthpieces have a narrower window than French mouthpieces. If you look through a German mouthpiece, you'll see that the side walls get slightly further apart towards the bottom of the chamber. *These angled side walls are said to make the sound,*

93

which is focused or centered by the narrow window, a bit 'broader.'
Straight side walls, on the other hand, are said to enhance the
projection and make the sound less warm.

Cord

The ligature is different too. German clarinetists still often bind
their reeds to the mouthpiece with a cord (see pages 84–85). In
order to provide the cord some extra hold, the mouthpiece has
grooves around it.

MOUTHPIECE BRANDS

There are quite a lot of mouthpiece makers. Many clarinet makers
make their own mouthpieces, others buy them from specializes
companies and print their own name on them. **Ernst Schreiber**
is one of the companies that supply other clarinet makers with
mouthpieces, besides marketing their own ESM mouthpieces.
The French **Vandoren** company, also known for the clarinet and
saxophone reeds, is one of the larger mouthpiece makers. Most
others are relatively small, specialized companies, including names
such as **Backun**, **Charles Bay**, **Behn**, **Bilger**, **Blayman**, **Brilhart**,
Combs, **Fobes**, **Guy Hawkins**, **J&D Hite**, **Jewel**, **Lakey**, **Otto Link**,
Meyer, **Mitchell Lurie**, **Morgan**, **Pomarico**, **Pyne**, **Rovner**, and
Wolf Tayne — and this list isn't even complete. Some of these
companies focus on high-end mouthpieces; others mainly produce
affordable models, or on mouthpieces in a wide range of prices.
Mouthpieces with a Viotto facing are made in Germany. Many
small mouthpiece makers use mouthpiece blanks by the German
company **Zinner** as the basis for their own products.

BARRELS

The barrel or *socket* is primarily used to tune the clarinet, but
it also has a significant influence on the sound, ease of playing,

94

and intonation of the instrument. Worthwhile investments can be made here, with a choice of affordable, standard after-market barrels and hand tuned, hand voiced barrels that are custom made for your instrument. Prices can go up to some three hundred dollars.

Two barrels

Many clarinets in the higher price ranges come with two barrels, one of them 0.40" or 0.80" (1 or 2 mm) longer than the other. The longer barrel makes the instrument sound just a little lower; the shorter one makes it sound a bit higher.

Shorter barrel, higher pitch

You might use that shorter barrel if you were playing with an orchestra that tunes slightly higher, or if it's very cold and your instrument is sounding a bit too low, or if you are a 'flat' clarinetist: Some clarinetists play slightly flatter than others, even with exactly the same instrument, mouthpiece, and reed. A shorter barrel can also compensate for the difference between your old mouthpiece and a new one that makes your instrument sound just a little flat — and vice versa.

Preferably longer

Some clarinetists prefer the longest barrel they can use while still playing in tune, because they say even those few tenths of an inch make their sound just a little deeper and warmer.

TIP

Too long, too short

The length of the barrel has a greater effect on the pitch of the notes from the upper part of the clarinet (the short-tube notes) than on the other notes. So if you choose a barrel that is too long, those short-tube notes will become much too low compared to the other notes. If your barrel is too short, on the other hand, the short-tube notes will be too high compared to the others. Barrels can be too long or too short even if they differ from the original barrel by some 0.060" (1.5 mm).

95

Adjustable

Adjustable barrels are also available. They usually go from approximately 2.35" to 3.25" (60–80 mm) in length. You can typically use no more than 0.120" (3 mm) of that range. If you extend it much further, or make it any shorter, the barrel becomes either too long or too short to still play in tune.

An adjustable barrel (Click Tuning Barrel).

Thick and thin

Separate barrels not only come in different lengths, but also in different shapes, wall thicknesses and materials, and with different bores. A barrel with a thicker wall gives a 'thicker,' darker, heavier, fuller sound. A clarinet with a thin wall barrel responds more easily, and has a brighter, lighter sound.

Materials

Besides barrels made of grenadilla, you can get all kinds of unusual designs in bronze, or wooden barrels with an ebonite lining for a somewhat brighter sound. Other types of wood are also used, such as cocobolo. This type of wood, with beautiful grain designs and a wide range of colors, is usually said to contribute to a warm, rich, full-bodied tone. For a rounder, darker sound you may try tulipwood, for example. Other types of wood

96

that are used for barrels — and bells, much to the same effect — include pearwood and boxwood.

Bore

The bore of the barrel is also important. Barrels with cylindrical bores promote a wider, more open sound than barrels whose bores narrow steadily toward the bottom: A *reverse taper* produces a warmer, more focused sound. There are many other variations, each of which has its own effect on the sound, the intonation (especially that of the short-tube notes), and the response of the instrument. Some barrels even have interchangeable bores.

> ## Ringless barrels and wooden rings
>
> *Most barrels have a metal ring on either side, as shown on page 6. Some specialized barrel designers also make ringless barrels, and barrels with wooden rings. The general reasoning is that metal rings tend to pinch the vibrations of the wood, making for a thinner overall tone quality. A ringless barrel allows for maximum vibrations, which also makes for a quick response and a free blowing feeling. Using wooden rings instead of metal rings is said to promote a fuller tone.*

Hard to predict

In the end, it will always be hard to predict how switching barrels will influence your timbre. The end result largely depends on how you play, your mouthpiece, the reed, and the instrument itself.

Barrel makers

Most clarinet makes produce their own barrels, of course. In addition, there are various smaller companies that specialize in barrels (or in barrels, bells, and mouthpieces, for example), such as Chadash, Fobes, Moennig, Backun, Segal, Vaccaro & Stevens, and Zinner.

97

NECKS

Larger clarinets, such as the alto and the bass, have a metal neck instead of a barrel. This neck or *bocal* is used to tune the instrument. Some necks consist of two sections that you fix together with a screw. Other types use cork tenons like a regular clarinet. Some makers supply one shorter and one longer neck to go with each instrument, just as you sometimes get two barrels with a soprano clarinet.

From the front

When you play a bass clarinet, the mouthpiece enters your mouth at a different angle to that of an ordinary clarinet: more from the front, instead of from below. That can make things difficult for clarinetists who play both instruments and often need to swap between them. A solution is to buy a special bass clarinet neck that is bent in such a way that the mouthpiece enters your mouth a little closer to the vertical.

With the special neck (right), the mouthpiece enters your mouth at a different angle.

traditional neck   modified neck

LIGATURES

Even the ligature contributes to your sound. The differences lie mainly in how the reed is held in place and in the material of the ligature.

One or two

Many ligatures have two screws. Although that takes a little more work, it does ensure a good distribution of pressure across the reed. Other ligatures have been designed to do the same job with a single screw.

98

Inverted

An *inverted ligature* has its screws on the other side of the ligature. This supposedly allows the reed to move more freely, and so respond more easily.

Material

Besides conventional metal ligatures, there are models in leather, soft plastic, textile, or metal mesh. The softer and thicker the material, the darker and more velvety the sound often becomes. The same happens if you secure the reed with a cord, as many German clarinetists do. A 'soft' ligature of this kind is also said to make the sound more flexible and darker.

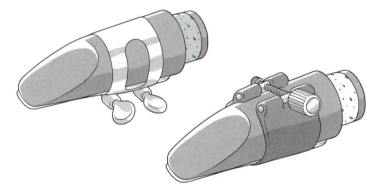

A metal ligature and a soft one.

Spots or strips

A very different effect is produced if the reed is held in place only by a few metal points or thin, metal strips. The less material touches the reed, the more freely it can vibrate; that usually makes the sound brighter and more open, and makes the instrument respond more easily. Other ligatures have adjustable clamp

TIP

Bite

Some types of ligature allow you to vary the exact position of the reed very easily, even without (re)moving the ligature itself. Others don't. Another difference is that some ligatures 'bite' into the reed. This means that you'll only be able to fix the reed in that same position from then on.

99

systems, so that you can adapt the sound to the music, the venue, or the ensemble.

Tips and tricks

You can also adjust simple ligatures to some extent. If you have a reed that is actually too light, tighten the upper screw a bit less. That allows a longer section of the reed to vibrate, which has an effect similar to that of a slightly heavier reed. There are more tips and tricks in Chapter 8, *Before and After.*

Prices

The least expensive standard ligatures are available for five to ten dollars. Expect to pay ten to twenty if you want something better, and twice to four times that amount if you want something special. Almost all clarinet and mouthpiece brands have their own ligatures, and there are also specialist brands such as BG, Oleg, Tru-Blo, and Winslow. A tip: A different ligature usually requires a different *mouthpiece cap.*

7

Reeds

What strings are to guitarists and violinists, reeds are to the clarinetist. They are important to the way you sound and the way you play. You need to replace them frequently, but there are all kinds of tricks to make them last as long as possible.

The main difference between one reed and the other is how soft or hard they are. Softer reeds are used mainly by beginners. To use a hard reed, which you'll find especially on mouthpieces with small tip openings, you need to be able to play well. You can tell how hard or soft a reed is by its number.

Numbers
Most manufacturers use the numbers 1 to 5, often in half steps. The higher the number, the harder or more resistant the reed.

TIP

> ### Beginners
> For beginners the best choice often is a soft to medium-soft reed, such as a 1.5 or a 2, on a mouthpiece with a tip opening of around 0.045–0.047" (1.15–1.19 mm).

Soft reeds
With a softer reed playing softly is easier. A soft reed speaks more easily, and it promotes a bright, lighter sound. On the other hand, softer reeds may sound thin and buzzy, and the may speak too easily. This can be a problem when trying to execute soft entrances in the upper register. Softer reeds also make it a little harder to play in perfect tune, as the pitch may go up and down as you play.

Reed and mouthpiece
Mouthpieces with a relatively large tip opening require relatively soft, flexible reeds. Conversely, smaller tip openings ask for harder reeds. For more information, see the section on mouthpieces in Chapter 6.

Harder reeds
Harder reeds allow for a louder, heavier, darker, or fuller sound, but they require strong breath support and a developed embouchure. Otherwise, these reeds tend to produce a stuffy, less desirable tone. Hard reeds also make it harder to play low pitches softly. Playing dynamics have less influence on the pitch, compared to soft reeds.

Equally thick

A higher number means that the reed is harder, being cut from
a harder, less flexible piece of cane. It will be exactly the same
thickness as a reed that has a lower number, assuming it's the same
type of reed.

Brands

Another tip: What one brand calls a number 2 may be equivalent
to a 1H or a 2H reed from another brand, and the same variation
can be found within different series of one brand. As with
mouthpieces, there are tables that list various brands and series
side by side. Some brands use names (i.e., soft, medium, hard, etc.)
instead of numbers.

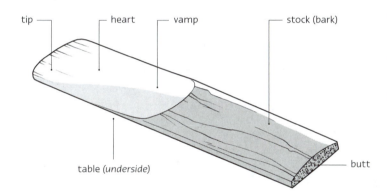

A reed
consists of
countless
hollow
miniature
tubes, as can
clearly be seen
at the butt.

Good reeds

Almost every box of reeds contains great reeds and good reeds,
average and poor ones. If the boxes you buy seem to contain fewer
and fewer good reeds, try a different brand or a different type
— and make sure that there isn't something else that causes the
problem. If your mouthpiece is damaged, for instance, no reed will
perform well.

Not equally hard

Of course, ten 'identical' reeds from one and the same box won't
all be equally hard either. A box of reeds number 2H will contain
reeds that are just a little harder than a 'hard' 2, as well as some
that come close to a 'soft' 3.

103

Thicker, steeper

How a reed plays and sounds also depends on its shape. The thickness of the heart may vary, the slope towards the edges may be a little steeper or a little more gentle, and so on. For example, some types of reeds are cut a little thicker to make for little tighter, clearer, or more focused sound.

Filed and unfiled

Reeds with a *file cut* or *double cut* have an extra strip of the bark removed, in a straight line, right behind the vamp area, as shown in the illustration. This allows for extra flexibility, promoting a faster response, a brighter and more focused tone, and making soft attacks easier.

Reeds without and with a (French) file cut.

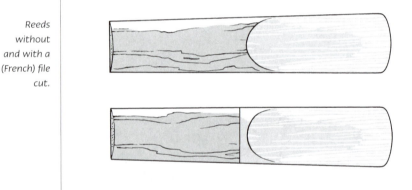

TIP

French

As this way of cutting reeds was developed in France — where classical players have always appreciated a brighter sound than in Germany, say — it's known as French file cut. The 'regular' or unfiled cut is sometimes referred to as single cut. Single cut reeds tend to promote a deeper sound.

Fine-tuning

The choice between filed and unfiled reeds can help you fine-tune your sound, regardless of the style in which you're playing. Generally speaking, players with a darker-sounding mouthpiece may prefer filed reeds, while unfiled reeds are often used on mouthpieces that tend to produce a brighter sound.

Which type of reed?

Each brand makes different types of reeds. The only way to find out which reed you like best is to keep trying them out. Trading experiences with other clarinetists helps, but every clarinetist plays differently, and a reed that works brilliantly with one mouthpiece can seem hopeless on another.

Still looking

So if you're still looking, buy reeds of different series, brands, and numbers. Try more than one reed of each type: One poor reed tells you nothing. Most clarinetists who have found 'their' reed buy them in boxes of five or ten. Reeds typically cost between one and a half to three dollars each.

German and Austrian reeds

The reeds you use for a German mouthpiece are cut differently than French reeds: They have a different profile. Some clarinetist say that you shouldn't use German reeds on a French mouthpiece, or the other way around. Still, others use — and love — such combinations. There are also special mouthpieces and reeds for Austrian (Viennese) players.

SELECTING REEDS

There are all kinds of ways to discover whether a reed is good or not so good, and there are all kinds of tricks to make reeds last as long as possible.

Against the light

If you hold up a reed to the light, you'll see an inverted V. That V must be precisely in the center of the reed, and the reed must get thinner evenly to the left and to the right. 'Crooked' reeds squeak, and they're hard to play.

| Good V-shape: can sound good. | A 'crooked' reed: risk of squeaks. | Uneven grain: better to avoid such reeds. | Knots: reed vibrates unevenly. |

Too young

A good reed is golden yellow to golden brown in color. Reeds with a hint of green are too young: Usually they won't play well, if at all, and won't last long.

Grain and knots

An even grain gives you a better chance of a reed that sounds good than a grain that crosses the reed at different angles. Reeds with spots and knots are unlikely to vibrate evenly.

Wet it first

You won't know how good a reed is until you have been playing it for a while. A dry reed doesn't vibrate properly, so always wet it first. Keep it in your mouth for a while or put it in a glass of lukewarm water for a few minutes. The latter method may extend the life of a reed: Some say water is better for reeds than saliva; others disagree.

Break them in

Reeds that perform very well straight away often don't last very long. The best reeds are often the ones that seem a little hard to begin with. In other words, they don't initially play well right away. That's why some clarinetists first 'break in' their new reeds, for instance by only using them a few minutes per day for the first week. They may also use that breaking-in period to adjust the reed if necessary, bit by bit, day by day. Other clarinetists never do: If a reed doesn't play well, they simply take a different one.

TIP

Double plus, double minus

When you're testing a box of new reeds, give each reed a grade, or give the best reeds two plusses, the worst ones two minuses, and so on. Don't throw away the 'bad' reeds, but leave them for a few months: Sometimes they will improve by themselves, and they never get too old. You can also try adjusting the poorer ones, or experiment a little with the placement of the reed on the mouthpiece (see page 120).

Swapping

Reeds are said to last longer if you don't use the same one for too long at a stretch. For that purpose, players may have a supply of good reeds on them, allowing them to switch reeds every hour or even sooner. If you use one reed all the time, it will gradually become weaker. By the time the reed 'goes,' it will be so weak that any new reed you try will seem too hard. Swapping helps prevent this.

Suddenly

If you switch reeds from time to time, you will also get a better feel for the little differences between reeds. What's more, you'll always have plenty of usable good reeds on hand — which is good, because even the best reed can give up suddenly.

Various playing conditions

You can also use these differences between individual reeds

(or even use different strengths or types of reeds) to adapt to various playing conditions. A harder-playing reed will help you compensate for high relative humidity, or to adapt your sound to very resonant or large venues. A lighter-playing reed works better in drier air, venues with dry acoustics, and small rooms. In other words: The reed that sounds great in a small, insulated practice studio may not be the best reed for your next concert.

TIP

> ### Tasty reeds
> *Don't you like the taste of cane? Then try some of the flavored reeds available, with a choice of raspberry, mint, grape, and other flavors, or treat your traditional reeds with a bottle of reed flavoring.*

ADJUSTING REEDS

Some clarinetists adjust every reed themselves, others do so only if it is really necessary, and many players don't do anything to their reeds at all. Learning to adjust reeds takes a lot of time and, to start with, a lot of reeds too. A few important tips are listed below. Some of the books on page 210 discuss this subject at greater length.

Higher, lower, or crooked
Before adjusting a reed, you can first experiment with its exact position on the mouthpiece. A reed that doesn't seem to work well when it is put on perfectly straight may suddenly start sounding good if you mount it a little higher, a little lower, or at a slight angle. Want to know more? See page 120.

Flat
If the facing of a reed (the part in contact with the mouthpiece) is not perfectly flat or even, you can sand it down. Lay a piece of very fine grade sandpaper (number 320 or finer) on a small plate

of glass, to make sure it is level, and draw the reed across it a few times.

Whetstone

Alternatively, you can get a whetstone (*carborundum stone*), or a dedicated reed surfacer. Move the reed over it lengthways along the grain of the reed, with smooth and even motions, or carefully sand it in a circular motion, both clockwise and counterclockwise. Exert as little pressure as possible and don't let the tip touch the stone. Some people scour the reed with a sharp penknife instead, pulling the blade across the reed a few times.

Tipcode CLR-010
This Tipcode demonstrates two ways to adjust a reed's facing.

TIPCODE

Too soft

A reed that's too soft can leave you with a messy, unsteady tone, or make a tone stop in midair. The solution is to clip off no more than 0.04" to 0.06" (1–1.5 mm) from the tip with a *reed cutter*

Tipcode CLR-011
A reed cutter is used to remedy a soft reed.

TIPCODE

109

or *reed trimmer.* First wet the reed. You may need to smooth the corners a little after cutting. Use a file, moving it towards the center of the reed, and only do so if it's necessary. Most reed cutters cost around twenty to fifty dollars.

Tip shape

A reed trimmer may also allow you to adapt the exact shape of the tip of your reed to the shape of the tip of your mouthpiece. Alternatively, you can do so with a sharp pair of scissors, but that requires a steady hand and quite some practice.

Too hard

If a reed is too hard, you can make it more flexible by scraping it with a sharp knife or a piece of *Dutch rush* or *reed rush*, for sale in music stores, or a synthetic replacement such as the Reed Stick. Start in the area around the figure 1. Do so very carefully, because the reed is already very thin at this point. If necessary, go on to the areas marked 2, then to 3 and 4. Always remove equal amounts left and right, otherwise you will push the reed out of balance.

Dutch rush or reed rush.

Tipcode CLR-012
This Tipcode shows you how to use Dutch rush.

Shrill or dull

You can try rescuing a shrill-sounding reed by adjusting the areas marked 3 and 4. On dull-sounding reeds you start at 1, then move on to 3 and 4, and possibly try 2 as well.

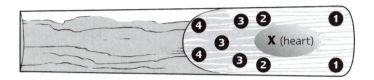

Squeak

Squeaking reeds are often not equally flexible or equally thick on the left and the right. In the latter case, you can try making the thicker edge a little thinner. Keep checking how much you have removed by blowing with the mouthpiece at an angle in your mouth: First try it left, then right.

Tips

- Work carefully: It's easy to remove **too much material**. For example, taking as little as 0.0004" (0.01mm) from the tip of a reed, makes it a whole 10% thinner!

- Frequently **check your results** as you work. Instead of constantly taking the ligature off and putting it back on again, you can also hold the reed in place with your thumb.

- Some reeds will **never be any good**, however much you work on them.

- As a rule, avoid the area marked X, the **heart of the reed**.

- If you want to tackle the job really seriously, you can buy special reed **adjustment devices and kits** with prices up to three hundred dollars.

- And finally: **Waves at the tip** of the reed will disappear when you play it for a while, or if you briefly put the reed in a glass of water.

111

LIFETIME

A reed consists of countless hollow miniature tubes or fibers with a soft material between them. This pulp or *pith* becomes gradually softer from exposure to your saliva, until it gets so soft that the reed stops working altogether. How long that takes depends on the type of saliva you have, how often you play, and on the reed itself. Reeds often last between two and four weeks, but there is this clarinetist who claims to have been using one specific reed for thirteen years, and only when performing Mozart in the summer…

 TIP

> ### Reed quality
> *How long a reed lasts, also depends on the quality of the cane that has been used. If for example the pith, mentioned above, has a very open texture, reeds tend to become spongy and soft relatively soon.*

Increasing the lifetime

There are all kinds of ways you can try to increase the useful life of your reeds.

- Rinse your reed in **clean water** after playing. Then dry it, for instance with a cotton cloth or handkerchief, or by passing it between your thumb and index finger, always towards the tip. Some clarinet players just dry the reed, without rinsing it first.

- **Hydrogen peroxide** solution (3%, available from your local drugstore) counteracts the effect of your saliva on the reed. Put your reeds in the solution overnight once in a while, and rinse them well before you use them again.

- Always store your reeds in a **good reed case or reed guard** (see pages 124–125).

- Lay each new reed on a flat surface and firmly rub it from the heart to the tip with the back of a teaspoon. This **closes the fibers** in the reed, which enhances its life expectancy.

- Don't play too long **without changing your reed**; swapping reeds works (see page 107).

- **Break your reeds in**, so that the dried material gradually gets used to being wet again.

- **Never** set down a mouthpiece with a reed in it vertically. Lay it on its side, so that it can't fall over. That'll save on broken reeds.

- **Taking a break**? A mouthpiece cap protects your reed and keeps it moist.

Synthetic reeds

As an alternative to cane reeds, various companies make synthetic or plastic reeds. These reeds are very consistent, and they last much longer than cane reeds. They're also insensitive to variations in humidity, making them very suitable for outdoor use. The fact that you don't have to wet them before playing makes synthetic reeds a serious option for musicians who play a variety of woodwinds in one show.

Sound

The first synthetic reeds were often said to sound shrill, harsh, or edgy, and they were usually considered to be a less than ideal choice for beginning players: They could be quite resistant and hard to control, next to producing problems. In later years, synthetic reeds were improved to the point that they have even gained acceptance in classical orchestras.

Brand names

Companies that market synthetic reeds include BARI, Fibracell, Hahn, Hartmann (Fiberreed), Légère, Olivieri, and RKM. Prices are typically around ten to twenty dollars a piece.

Plastic coated reeds

As an alternative for synthetic reeds, there are plastic coated cane reeds such as the Rico Plasticover. Basically, these reeds offer the same advantages as synthetic reeds do, but at a lower price and with a shorter life expectancy. Coated reeds tend to offer a quick response and a clear tone with great projection.

113

Some brand names

The American **Rico** company also makes reeds for their **LaVoz**, **Hemke** en **Mitchell Lurie** brand names. **Vandoren**, the French company that was mentioned before as a mouthpiece maker, is one of the other main names in reeds. **Brancher**, **Glotin**, **Marca**, and **François Louis** are also French; most of the reed cane grows in that country (see page 157), but there are also plantations in Mexico, Argentina (where **Gonzalez** reeds are made), and other countries. Two relatively young names are **Alexander Superial** (Japan) and **Reeds Australia**. Reeds are also made in Germany (**Steuer**, **Willscher**, **Hafner**) and Italy (**Lucien**, **Bonazza**). **Prestini** was founded in Italy. The American company also makes pads and instruments. Other brand names include **Ponzol** and **Zonda**.

8

Tuning and Accessories

A chapter about all the things you need to do with your clarinet before and after playing: from putting it together and warming it up to tuning it, taking it apart, and drying and storing it, including tips on amplification, stands and lyres. More advanced maintenance is discussed in Chapter 9.

A lot of clarinets get broken by falling out of cases that have been opened the wrong way up. So before opening the case, make sure the lid is at the top. A tip: The lid usually has a logo on it. If not, you can tell which way up the case is by looking at the handle, which is always attached to the bottom half.

Cracks

Wooden clarinets can crack due to rapid changes in temperature and air humidity. If you've been outdoors on a very cold day and you then walk into a warm room, you should allow your clarinet to acclimatize in its case first. You can also warm it up in your hands. Don't start playing until the instrument no longer feels cold to the touch, so that the moisture and warmth of your breath won't shock the material.

Only one way

There's usually only one way to put a clarinet back into its case. Exactly how depends on the design of the case — so have a good look before taking the instrument out. Be especially careful with the upper and lower joints, to avoid bending the keys. One tip: The keys must always face up.

TIP

Cork grease

Cork grease makes everything slide more smoothly when you're assembling your clarinet, it keeps the cork of the tenons in good condition, and seals the joints better. You can get it in small bottles or in lipstick-style containers, the latter keeping your fingers cleaner. Apple-scented cork grease and other aromas are also available.

Gently

There are all kinds of ways to assemble a clarinet. One commonly used method is described below. A tip before you start: Don't lift the upper and lower joints out of the case by the keywork. Instead, use a finger to gently lift them up a little by one end, and then get hold of them properly.

116

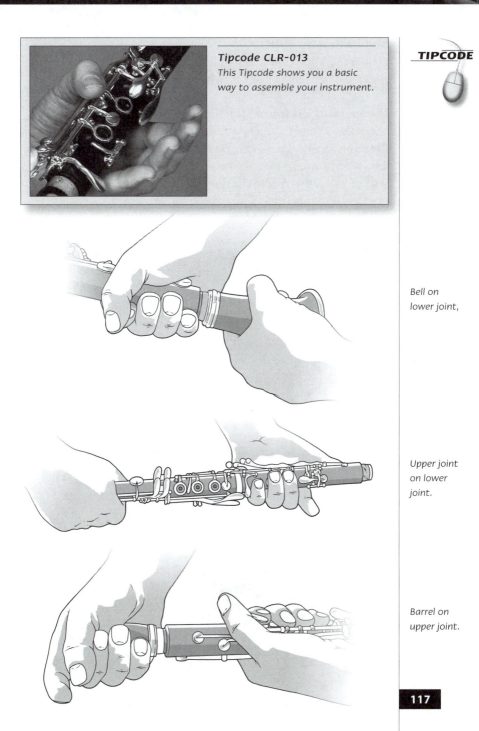

Tipcode CLR-013

This Tipcode shows you a basic way to assemble your instrument.

TIPCODE

Bell on lower joint,

Upper joint on lower joint.

Barrel on upper joint.

117

Bell on lower joint

First take the lower joint. Hold it as shown in the illustration and attach the bell with a careful twisting movement.

Upper joint on lower joint

Now take hold of the upper joint, resting your fingers on the rings. Press the ring keys down as you attach the upper joint to the lower joint with a careful twisting movement. Hold the lower joint at the bottom end, as shown in the illustration, without squeezing the mechanism. The bell will give you some extra grip.

The bridge

To avoid damaging the bridge mechanism, it should be in the 'open' position when you are joining the upper and lower joints together. This is why you should press down the ring keys of the upper joint and *not* press the ones of the lower joint.

Hold down the D/A ring, so that the bridge is in the open position as you slide the upper and lower joints together.

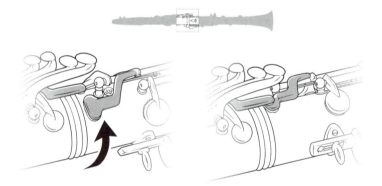

TIPCODE

Tipcode CLR-014
When assembling your instrument, the bridge should be open. Here's how you do that.

118

Barrel on upper joint

Now slide the barrel onto the upper joint. The easiest way is to rest the bell on the top of your leg, so that you don't have to grip the clarinet too tightly.

Mouthpiece

Again, rest the bell against your leg to help you slide the mouthpiece onto the barrel. Next, fit the reed.

In four steps

1. Slide the ligature over the mouthpiece until it's almost in its final position.

2. Place the wetted reed (see page 106) under the ligature...

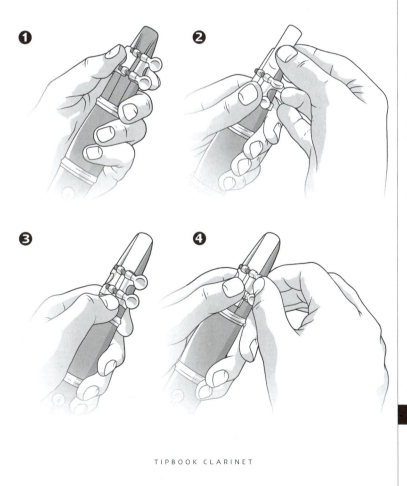

❶   ❷

❸   ❹

1. First the ligature...

2. ... then the reed.

3. Check its position...

4. ... then tighten the ligature.

119

3. … and make sure the edges and the tip are exactly in line with the rails and tip of the mouthpiece.

4. Now slide the ligature into place and tighten it carefully. If you tighten it too much, the reed won't vibrate properly.

TIPCODE

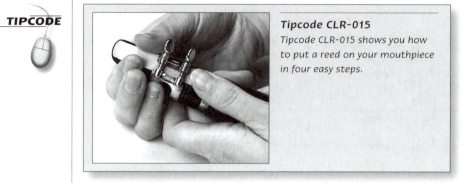

Tipcode CLR-015
Tipcode CLR-015 shows you how to put a reed on your mouthpiece in four easy steps.

Better
If a reed feels too hard, set it a little lower down the mouthpiece. If it feels very light, try moving it up a bit, or try sliding the ligature down slightly, or loosening the upper screw a little. Reeds that are not perfectly even left and right will often perform better if you set them on your mouthpiece at a slight angle.

In line
Mouthpiece, upper and lower joints must all be in line. You can usually tell whether they are by looking at the brand name, if it

… a catch for the upper and lower joints…

is shown on all the sections. Alternatively, you can look along the underside of the instrument, from the bell to the reed. Some clarinets have special catches to make sure the upper and lower joints are always in line.

Everything in line? Look along the underside of the instrument.

Brushing and flossing, food and drinks

If you want to make it as easy as possible to keep your clarinet clean, both inside and out, wash your hands and brush and floss your teeth before you play, don't eat during intermissions, and don't drink anything that contains sugar.

TUNING

Like most other instruments, a clarinet needs to be tuned before you start playing. The usual method of tuning is to pull the upper joint and barrel apart by some 0.04" to 0.08" (1–2 mm). A clarinet that sounds too low can only be tuned by using a shorter barrel.

Concert A

Most orchestras and bands tune to concert A (see page 54). On a B♭ clarinet that means you finger a B.

Tuning fork

If you have a piano or another keyboard instrument handy, you can sound concert A by playing the A just to the right of the center (A4). The same note will sound if you use a tuning fork in A. Just tap this small, thick fork against your knee, say, before setting the stem against your ear. Tuning forks are also available in other tunings (see page 54). Electronic tuners and metronomes can often play this A too.

TIPCODE

Tipcode CLR-005 and CLR-016
Tipcode CLR-005, again, plays the reference pitch A=440. The use of a tuning fork is demonstrated in Tipcode CLR-016. This particular fork also sounds A=440.

To other notes
In some groups it may be preferred to tune to other notes. The open G, for instance (concert F), or the D (concert C), because it is thought to be more stable than the B. Groups with many brass instruments (e.g., concert bands and marching bands), most of which are pitched in B♭, often tune to C (concert B♭).

Barrel and upper joint
Quite often, tuning is simply a matter of pulling the barrel and upper joint apart slightly. However, that isn't always enough, because when you pull the barrel and upper joints apart, the short-tube notes go down further than the long-tube notes — just as they would when using a longer barrel (see pages 95–96).

The rest
If you also pull apart the upper and lower joints slightly, the notes that go down the most are the highest notes of the lower joint. By pulling out the bell a little, you can fine-tune the long-tube notes. If you are playing together with other clarinetists, it's usually best if you all use the same tuning procedure.

Different notes
Because each clarinet has certain notes that tend to sound flat or

sharp, you should never tune to just one note. For instance, if you tune to an open G, you might try also playing the higher- and lower-sounding E and B (the notes of the E-minor chord) and listening to whether the distances between those notes are correct. If you are tuning to a C, you could also play the E and G (C-major chord).

Groove

When you pull two sections of a clarinet apart, a groove will be formed between them. Not only on the outside, but on the inside of the tube too. This groove can cause the sound to deteriorate slightly. Moreover, condensation collects easily in the groove, and the groove increases the effects of tuning: When you pull the barrel out, the pitch of the short-tube notes will be even lower.

Tuning rings

The solution is to use *tuning rings*, which you place inside the tenons to fill up this groove. Tuning rings are usually sold in sets of two or three rings in various thicknesses (i.e., 0.5, 1.0, and 2.0 mm), costing about five to ten dollars.

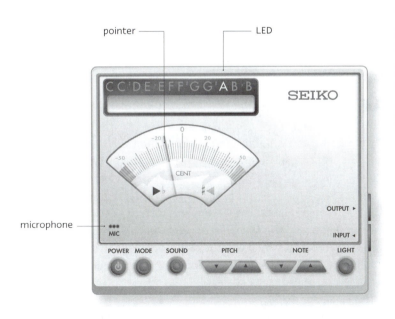

An automatic, chromatic electronic tuner. The A it hears, sounds a little flat.

Some do, some don't

Some clarinetists swear by tuning rings; other don't use them, because the rings need to be taken out if you want to tune to a higher pitch, or because they may start buzzing when you tune the clarinet a bit lower.

Tuners

An electronic tuner can be useful to tune your clarinet. Its built-in microphone 'hears' the note you are playing and tells you whether the pitch is sharp, flat or exactly right. *Tip:* Most tuners automatically switch off after a couple of minutes, which saves on batteries.

TIP

> ## Higher temperature, higher pitch
>
> *After you've been playing for a while, your instrument will gradually warm up. This makes the tuning go up, so that after five to ten minutes' playing you'll often need to retune slightly. The better you warm up the instrument prior to playing, the less retuning will be necessary. Warming up your instrument is simply a matter of playing it, or blowing warm air through it, without making the reed vibrate.*

AFTER

If you never clean your clarinet, the first thing you'll notice is that your mouthpiece starts smelling funny. Try to prevent that.

Reed

Reeds last longest if you rinse them and then dry them after playing (see page 112). If you leave your reed on the mouthpiece, it won't dry as easily, which will make it more likely to warp. Besides, you'll have to take it off to wet it next time you play anyway.

Reed cases

You can store the reed in a very basic open reed holder or in a reed guard, available for a couple of dollars, or get yourself a deluxe, leather-clad reed case for fifty dollars, or something in between.

Special cases

Your reeds will dry most evenly in a reed case with ventilation holes and a ribbed floor, so that the air can get everywhere. Other cases have glass floors that help to prevent waves forming at the tip of the reed. What works best may depend on the reeds you use, and on how wet or dry they are when you store them.

Moisture control

Some holders have replaceable cartridges containing a substance that keeps the humidity at the right level. The Rico Reed Vitalizer and the Vandoren Hygrocase are designed to that same effect.

Numbered

Some reed cases and holders have numbered compartments, so you can tell the reeds apart. This is especially useful if you often change reeds or if you use different reeds for different situations.

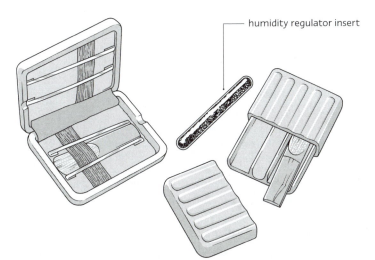

humidity regulator insert

Various reed guards.

Drying

Before you put your clarinet away, you need to dry it: That's better for the wood and for the pads. First, take the mouthpiece off and (ideally) rinse it in lukewarm water before you dry it, using a handkerchief or a special cloth.

125

Swabs

Next dry the rest of the clarinet with a *swab*: a cloth with a cord and a weight attached to it. First lower the weight into the tube, then pull the cloth through the instrument.

TIPCODE

Tipcode CLR-017
A swab can be used from the bell up, or the other way around, or both up and down.

From the bell upwards

The barrel is the part that gets the wettest, so it would seem logical to pull the cloth through the instrument from the bell upwards. All the same, some clarinetists prefer to do it the other way round (or both!), and some prefer to dry their instruments joint by joint. If you decide to do it that way, take the clarinet apart, lay the sections in the case, and take them out again one by one to dry them.

TIP

Caught

A swab can easily get caught behind the register tube or the thumbhole tube. Free it by pulling it back a little way in the other direction.

Tenons, toneholes, and pads

Don't forget to dry the tenons. Condensation often collects there, as it does in the toneholes. If the toneholes are wet, your pads won't make a proper seal. Sometimes you can dry toneholes simply by blowing on them from the outside. Otherwise, blow hard through the lower or upper joint. There are various way to dry wet pads (see page 130).

126

Cotton or chamois

Most swabs have cotton cloths, but some have cloths made of chamois leather, silk, or wool. Cotton cloths need to be washed regularly, even when they are new: New cotton doesn't dry as well as old. Chamois, on the other hand, should not be washed.

A pull-through swab.

Pad saver

Some clarinetists prefer to use a *pad saver*, a long fluffy plume that you stick into your clarinet after drying it. Others prefer not to, because pad savers leave behind fibers that can stick to the pads, because many don't absorb the moisture but spread it around, or because they may have metal rods that can damage the bore. Yet another alternative is a cloth-covered rod, which can be used to dry and clean the bore of the instrument.

Side pocket

The best place to keep your swab is in a side pocket of your case. If you store it in or with your clarinet, pads and springs can be affected by the moisture in the cloth.

TIP

Wait a while

If you can't easily take your clarinet apart after playing it, let it cool down for a while. If that doesn't help, don't use a wrench or undue force but wrap it in a towel (it will no longer fit inside its case) and take it to a technician.

127

Locked

Some cases have lids that automatically click shut when you close the case. If yours doesn't, always make sure you close the lid properly before you pick up the case. Too many clarinets have fallen out of unclosed cases.

AND IN BETWEEN

When you take a break, put the cap on the mouthpiece, and make sure your clarinet can't get damaged. It may be best to put the instrument on a clarinet stand. That way it will hardly take up any space. A clarinet stand also helps to prevent people from sitting down on or stepping on your instrument.

Folding stands

You can buy a compactly folding clarinet stand for as little as ten to twenty dollars. The longer its feet are, the less chance there is that someone will knock it over. On some stands, the cone that the clarinet slides onto is covered with felt, which protects the bore against scratches and wear.

A clarinet stand that easily folds up to a very small size.

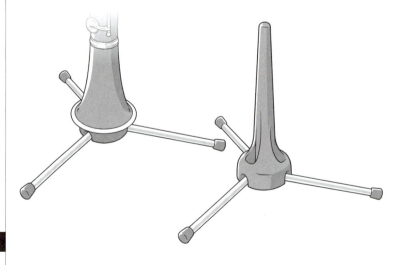

Heat

Never leave a clarinet where it will get too hot or too dry. Watch out for heaters, radiators, direct sunlight, air conditioning vents, and other dangerous spots.

Splutter

If you hear a spluttering sound on certain notes, it's probably due to moisture in a tonehole. The toneholes of the C♯/G♯ key and the trill keys are especially sensitive to this problem, due to their position on the instrument: The moisture in the tube tends to run in their direction. Try to remove the moisture by blowing into the instrument very hard, or by blowing it off from the outside. Otherwise, slide a piece of pad cleaning paper between the pad and the tonehole, so it can absorb the moisture. This type of paper is available at your music store, where they also sell Pad Cleaner and similar products.

Cigarette paper

Cigarette paper has always been an effective alternative for pad cleaning paper, but it's not always easily available. If you use it, make sure the gummed edge stays away from your pads. You can also use a small section of a paper coffee filter, should you still have that type of filter around.

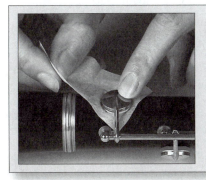

TIPCODE

Tipcode CLR-018
Tipcode CLR-018 shows you how to use a piece of cleaning paper to treat your pads.

Oil

The pad of the C♯/G♯ key is especially prone to becoming waterlogged. Some technicians prevent the problem by drawing a line of oil alongside or around the tonehole in question. The idea is that the moisture will follow the oil and not end up in the tonehole.

Sticky pads

Sticky or damp pads — which you'll often find at the same keys — can be cleaned with pad cleaning paper or cigarette paper. Slide the paper under the pad, and hold the key closed for a little while. No improvement? Take a clean piece of paper, drip one or two drops of lighter fuel or an alcohol-based cleaning fluid onto it, and repeat the steps above. Dry the pad with a fresh piece of paper afterwards. Be careful when using lighter fuel or alcohol: both are highly flammable.

Preferably not

It's better not to clean or dry pads with talcum powder or other kinds of powder, banknotes, newspaper, or anything else that has been printed. If you have leather pads, you can use paper tissues to clean them.

Loose springs

If a key stops working, its spring may have come loose. Usually, it's quite easy to put it back into place. If the spring of a closed key is missing, you may be able to play on by holding the key shut with a rubber band. A tip: Take the rubber band off after playing and don't store any in your case. Rubber contains substances that are harmful to silver. Another tip: For the same reason, don't store erasers in your case.

Loose tenons

Sometimes the cork on one or several of the tenons is so badly worn away that it doesn't grip or seal anymore. A temporary solution is to twist a cigarette paper or some yarn around it, but it's better to get the tenons recorked.

CASES AND BAGS

Most new clarinets come with their own case or bag, but these accessories are available separately too.

Five pieces
In most cases and bags you store your clarinet in five pieces: mouthpiece + cap + ligature as one, and then barrel, upper joint, lower joint, and bell. Others make you store it in two or three (very rarely), four (the bell stays on the lower joint) or more parts.

Hard-shell cases
Hard-shell cases usually have a molded plastic or plywood core and a plush lining. French-style cases, which have no handle, are often used in combination with a separate case cover in canvas,

Gig bag with backpack straps; clarinet case.

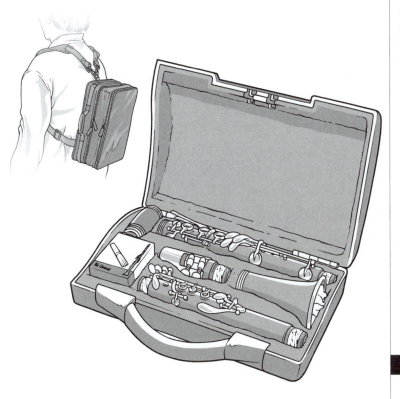

131

Cordura, or leather, for example. There are also hard-shell clarinet cases that look like a regular briefcase, concealing the fact that you are carrying a musical instrument.

Bags

The same goes for so-called *carryall bags*, which have shoulder straps and lots of extra space that you can use for a music stand, sheet music, and other bits and pieces. *Gig bags* are soft 'cases' with heavily padded sides. They usually come with an accessory pocket, a sheet music compartment, and adjustable backpack straps that offer a safe way to transport a clarinet when biking or walking.

Space

If you are buying a new case or bag, check how much extra storage space it offers. Will you be able to fit a box of reeds and a reed guard in it, or a second mouthpiece, an extra barrel, cork grease,

TIP

Prices

Cases and bags are available from around forty dollars. If you want a luxury version, with a wooden shell, leather covering, and space for two clarinets (e.g., A and B♭), you can easily spend ten times that amount.

A clarinet lyre.

132

or a neckstrap? Does it have a side pocket for your swab, a music stand, a lyre, or sheet music?

Lyre

Marching clarinetists put their sheet music on a *lyre*, which will fit on the instrument without the use of drills or screws. Some lyres offer a separate attachment point for a neckstrap. Most lyres are designed to be attached half way up the clarinet. Lyres that are attached at the bell make it harder to read the music.

AMPLIFICATION

The clarinet is a very dynamic instrument, but if you play it in a band with electric instruments and a drummer, you will soon need to be amplified.

Wind instrument microphones

Most microphone companies have special wind instrument microphones. These may not look very different from vocal microphones, but they are. Two examples:

- Instrument microphone are built to handle the **higher sound pressure level** (SPL) of a wind instrument.

- Vocal microphones have a built-in **pop filter** that reduces the 'explosions' you create when singing so-called plosive consonants (e.g., P, B, T). When used for a wind instrument, this filter tends to cancel out essential frequencies.

Pickup pattern

Microphones come with different *pickup patterns*, which refers to how they respond to sounds coming from different directions. For instruments such as the clarinet, a microphone with a heart-shaped or cardioid pickup pattern, tends to be the best choice if you want to pick up the natural sound of the instrument. A microphone with a super cardioid pattern is less sensitive for feedback, but it produces a more direct, less natural sound.

133

Small membrane

Most wind instrument microphones are small-membrane condenser microphones. If you want to know what that means, please check out *Tipbook Amplifiers and Effects* (see page 236).

Stand-mounted microphones

Using a stand-mounted microphone limits your freedom of movement. If you move the instrument away from the microphone, the volume will decrease. Moving too close can make for a boomy sound due to the mic's *proximity effect*. You can use all of this to your advantage, increasing the dramatic effect and the dynamic range of the instrument, but it's often easier to use a dedicated clarinet-mounted microphone.

A clarinet with two dedicated clip-on microphones

Clip on

Various companies make special clip-on clarinet microphone systems that are designed to capture all elements of the sound. An isolated mounting helps reduce the amplification of mechanic sounds and contact noise.

Pre-amp

These systems usually feature condenser microphones. The power that this type of microphone needs is usually supplied by a small,

Try them out

Just like clarinets, microphones all have their own sound. Whether you buy a stand-mounted microphone or a clip-on system, always try out various models, preferably with your own instrument.

typically belt-worn preamplifier, which also allows you to adjust volume and other parameters.

Prices

Prices for these systems range from about three to five hundred dollars, but you may find systems that cost even less. Wireless systems are more expensive.

Amps and effects

If you use a microphone more often than not, you may consider purchasing your own amp too, and possible some types of effects that help enhance your sound. More information on these products, microphones, cables, wireless systems and related subjects can be found in *Tipbook Amplifiers and Effects* (again, see page 236).

ON THE ROAD

- Don't put a clarinet on the **luggage shelf of a car**, under the rear window — especially not on a hot day.

- Getting **out of the car**? Always take your instrument with you.

- All kinds of things — including clarinets — get left behind in the luggage racks of buses, trains, and subways. *Tip:* Always **keep hold of your instrument**.

- If you still leave your clarinet behind somewhere, you're more likely to get it back if your **name, (email) address, and phone number** are listed inside your case or bag.

135

- Consider **insuring your instrument**, especially if you take it on the road. This includes visiting your teacher. Musical instruments fall under the insurance category of 'valuables.' A regular homeowners' insurance policy will usually not cover all possible damage, whether it occurs at home, on the road, in the studio, or onstage.

- To get your instrument insured you'll need to know the **serial number** and some other details. There is space for that information on pages 230–231. Insurance companies may also ask for an appraisal report (see page 37) and proof of purchase.

9

Maintenance

If you always do everything you read in the previous chapter, your clarinet won't need much additional maintenance. A bit of extra cleaning now and again, and perhaps the odd drop of oil. That's all there is to it. Once in a while, though, you will need to take your clarinet to a technician for a COA (cleaning, oiling, and adjustment) or an overhaul.

Even if you always use a swab to dry your mouthpiece after playing, it will need extra cleaning from time to time. Use cold or lukewarm water. A special mouthpiece brush is a useful tool. Remove chalk scale with a mouthpiece cleaner, which will also disinfect the mouthpiece. As an alternative, you may consider using ordinary vinegar to remove chalk. Be careful not to soak you ebonite mouthpiece in vinegar, though: It will make it turn green (and do note that hot water may do the same!). Instead, soak some cotton wool in vinegar and put it inside the mouthpiece, without wetting the visible outside. Leave it in for a quarter of an hour. If bits of chalk remain, try rubbing them off with a cotton bud. Don't use sharp tools. Carefully rinse the mouthpiece afterwards to avoid a vinegar taste.

Toothpaste
Some players use toothpaste, but that will soon be too abrasive. Others have removed scale and other deposits by putting their mouthpiece in soda (e.g., coke) overnight.

Polishing the keywork
A nickel-plated mechanism needs no more than a shine with a dry cloth. If you have a silver-plated mechanism, you can use a silver polishing cloth to clean it and restore its luster. Don't use it too often, though: The built-in polishing agent will eventually wear through the plating.

TIP

Black
If your silver-plated keywork tarnishes faster than you can polish it (see page 41), you're better off getting an instrument with a nickel-plated mechanism, or having the mechanism gold-plated. A sudden discoloration of the keywork can be caused by something in your diet, such as spinach or eggs, certain medicines, erasers or rubber bands in your case, or even a new ebonite mouthpiece. If your mouthpiece seems to be the guilty party, store it in a plastic bag outside the case for the first few weeks.

No ordinary polish

Ordinary silver and metal polishes tend to be too abrasive for musical instruments: They can damage your pads, and residue may get into the hinges, gumming up the keywork. To be avoided, in other words.

Oiling the mechanism

The best way to oil the mechanism is to take it apart completely — so it's best to leave this to a technician. If only a few of the keys need to be lubricated, and you decide to do it yourself, use as little oil as possible. First dip a match or a pin into a little oil on a saucer or a piece of paper; then apply it to the hinge. Use special clarinet key oil from your music store, not whatever you happen to have at home. Two tips: Oil is disastrous for pads, and don't oil a mechanism that already works smoothly.

Cleaning

The best way to clean the little nooks and crannies of the mechanism is with a small, clean (paint) brush. The more often you do this, the less chance that dust and dirt will lodge there.

Play

When you're polishing the mechanism, check levers and keys for play. If you find keys or levers that move in directions they shouldn't, this may be simply due to a loose screw, but play can also be caused by wear. Of the latter seems to be the case, have your instrument checked by a technician: If you don't, it'll get worse.

> **Toneholes**
> Even if you always play with clean hands, the edges of the open toneholes will eventually become dirty. There are special cleaning sticks available. Q-Tips will do too, as long as you make sure that the cotton fibers don't end up in the keywork or the instrument.

TIP

Rings

Now and then, check whether the bell ring, tenon rings, and body rings are still tight. Loose rings can cause buzzes. They also show

139

that the wood has shrunk, indicating that the clarinet has been stored in conditions that are too dry. Air conditioning and central heating systems are two of the main causes of dry air. An air humidity level of 40 to 60 percent is usually considered good for both musical instruments and human beings.

OILING THE BORE

There are few things clarinetists disagree about as strongly as oiling the bores of wooden clarinets. Some do it every three months, while others haven't used oil for decades and never had problems. Some factories recommend that you oil a new clarinet, others advise against it. The simplest tip? Ask for advice when you buy your instrument, or leave it to your technician.

Cracks
Most experts believe that a thin film of oil in the bore reduces the risk of cracks. Others say that grenadilla is so hard and strong that oil could never prevent a clarinet from cracking. The only thing that can be said for sure is that wooden clarinets sometimes crack, whether or not they have been frequently oiled.

The best way
Oil hardly penetrates the wood, if at all, but leaves behind a thin, protective film. The best way to oil the bore is to first allow the instrument to dry thoroughly. Then remove the mechanism, oil the wood, clean the toneholes, reassemble the instrument, and adjust it. A job for a professional, in other words.

Easier
The easiest way to oil the bore is to dry the instrument as well as you can, put pieces of cling film under all the pads, put a very small amount of oil on a special cleaning rod, and move it backwards and forwards through the tube a few times. An important tip: It's easier to damage a clarinet by using too much oil than by using too little.

Almond oil and bore oil

There are special bore oils for sale, and sweet almond oil is often used as well. These types of oil don't dry, which means they easily get wiped off and you would have to use them quite often.

Hard oil or wax

Linseed oil and tung oil do dry, so they stay on longer. These 'hard' oil types are best applied by an expert. Why? For one thing, if you use a bit too much you can end up with a crusty, gel-like layer inside your clarinet. Rather than oil, some players use beeswax.

SERVICE AND OVERHAULS

New clarinets need to be checked and adjusted after six months to a year. In some cases, that first service is included in the purchase price.

Cleaning, oiling, and adjusting

If you get your clarinet checked once a year, you can be fairly sure that nothing major can go wrong. Some technicians consider once every two years to be sufficient, depending on how much you play. Expect to pay some fifty to seventy-five dollars for an annual checkup or COA (cleaning, oiling, adjusting). The longer you wait, the more expensive it can get.

Overhaul

Clarinets need to be overhauled once every five to ten years. If you choose, you can have your instrument made as good as new, with new pads, new tenons, new silver-plating, new springs, new rods, new screws, and so on. The price will depend on what needs to be done, but also on the quality and age of the clarinet.

Try it out

Whether you take your instrument for a COA or a full overhaul, it will be adjusted. A tip: Try your instrument out before you take it

141

home again, so that you know that it plays the way you want it to. Adjustment is a very personal thing, after all. On the other hand: You may have to get used to the instrument feeling differently, especially if the adjustment was way off.

10.

History

If you read ten books on the history of the clarinet, chances are each will tell a different story — and no one knows who's right. Everybody does agree, however, that the earliest predecessors of the instrument date back some five thousand years, and that the clarinet itself is about three hundred years old.

To find the very first predecessors of the clarinet you have to go back at least until ancient Egypt, where they were playing the *memet* as long ago as 3000 BC.

Idioglottic

The memet had an *integral reed*: The reed is cut from the tube itself, staying attached to it at one end only. This makes the memet an *idioglottic instrument*.

One tube or two

The clarinet had many other ancestors and early family members, such as the Greek *aulos*, the Chinese *cuen kan*, the ancient Arabian *arghul*, and the Welsh *pibcorn* or *hornpipe*: All instruments with a single reed, many with one tube, some with two.

Chalumeau

The chalumeau was another single-reed instrument. According to some experts, the chalumeau was first played two thousand years ago; others regard the Middle Ages as more likely. Some expert books will tell you that not a single chalumeau has been preserved, while other, equally scholarly works show actual photographs of the instrument.

Register key

The most important difference between the chalumeau and the first clarinets is the register key. Missing this key, the chalumeau had a range no larger than — of course — the chalumeau register of the modern clarinet.

Clarinet

With the introduction of the register key the range of the instrument was extended considerably. The new, higher register in some ways resembled the sound of a trumpet, and so the clarinet got its name; the word clarinet is derived from the Italian word for trumpet, *clarino*, or small trumpet, *clarinetto*.

Denner and Sons

It is unclear who exactly invented the register key, and hence the clarinet. Most sources do agree that the inventor was

144

called Denner. Some experts claim it was the Nuremberg instrument maker Johann Christian Denner; others say it must have been one of his sons, because the clarinet is first mentioned in 1710, three years after the death of Denner Senior.

Five to six keys

Gradually, the clarinet acquired more keys: Without those extra keys, you would only be able to play it in a few different key signatures. Around 1800, most clarinets had around five or six keys.

Iwan Müller

In 1812, the clarinetist Iwan Müller produced a clarinet with thirteen keys, enough to play it in any key signature. Those thirteen keys were not the only ace up Müller's sleeve: He also used a metal ligature, and he was one of the first clarinetists to turn the mouthpiece upside down. Before then, the instrument was played with the reed facing upwards.

Bärmann and Oehler

Half a century later, Carl Bärmann added a further five or six keys to the Müller clarinet, and another fifty-odd years after that, Oskar Oehler used Bärmann's design as the basis for his own clarinet system, which most German professionals still play today.

Albert and Sax

Improvements on Müller's work were being made in Belgium, too, by among others Eugène Albert, after whom the 'German' Albert system is named. Another famous Belgian who occupied himself with the clarinet was Adolphe Sax, who invented the 'sax-o-phone' around 1840.

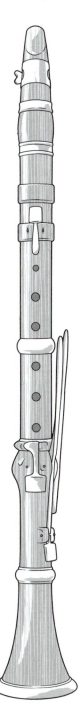

Boxwood clarinet in C with five keys and ivory body rings (Savary, Paris, 1780; collection Jac. Schaap).

145

Klosé and Buffet

Around the same time, the Frenchmen Hyacinte Klosé and Louis Auguste Buffet were also working on the clarinet. Put simply, they took some of the ideas of Theobald Boehm, the inventor of the modern (Boehm) flute, and applied them to the clarinet. Boehm himself had nothing else to do with their clarinet, but the instrument was nevertheless named after him.

Perfect, or not?

Since Albert, Oehler, and the first Boehm clarinets, nothing much has changed. Some experts say that is a good thing, since they consider the modern clarinet to be a perfect instrument. Others feel the clarinet is still in its infancy stage, because there's so much left to be improved — and the number of custom made bells and barrels may prove them right.

11

The Clarinet Family

The immediate clarinet family consists of at least thirteen clarinets in different tunings. All kinds of other instruments with single reeds are also related, and if you include all the members of the woodwind family of instruments, you need to add the saxophone, the flute, the oboe, and others.

Clarinets come in all kinds of tunings. The most popular is of course the soprano clarinet in B♭, followed by the soprano clarinets in A (slightly larger, and lower in pitch) and E♭ (shorter, and higher), and there are also sopranos in C and D. The E♭ instrument is so much smaller that it often doesn't have separate upper and lower joints.

A few in A♭ and C

Smaller still, and much rarer, are the sopranino clarinets. There are two of them: in A♭ and in C.

Basset clarinet

The *basset clarinet* is an extended soprano clarinet in A. Because of the extra length the lowest note is a C, instead of the usual E. The basset clarinet is often used for Mozart's famous clarinet concerto, which is why it is sometimes known as a *Mozart clarinet*.

Basset horn

The modern *basset horn*, pitched in F, most closely resembles an alto clarinet. The German version has the basset keys, which are operated with the right thumb, at the back of the instrument, while the French version has them at the front. Earlier basset horns came in many different models; one of them had a semi-circular tube, which explains the 'horn' part of its name.

Contra-alto, contrabass, and sub-contrabass

If you want to go lower still, you need a *contra-alto clarinet* (E♭) or a *contrabass clarinet* (B♭). These instruments sound an octave lower than the alto clarinet and the bass clarinet respectively. Both come in various models, some featuring a straight wooden, metal or plastic tube, others a coiled metal tube with two bows in it. The curves make these long instruments a bit shorter, so you don't need to stand up to play them. Finally, there's the extremely rare *sub-contrabass clarinet*, which sounds another octave lower than the contrabass.

Harmony clarinets

All clarinets larger or smaller than the soprano are often collectively called *harmony clarinets*: In many orchestras and

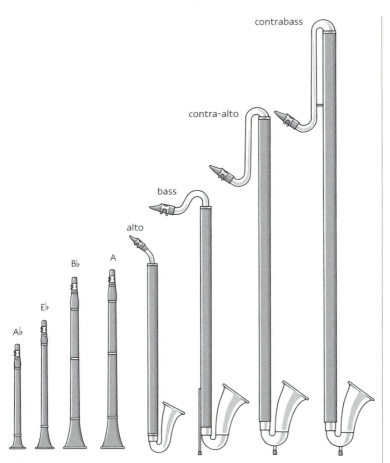

contrabass

contra-alto

bass

alto

A

B♭

E♭

A♭

ensembles they are used to play the harmonies that accompany the soloist or the melody.

Turkish and Greek in G
There are many other varieties of clarinet. One example would be the metal soprano clarinet in G that is often used in Turkish and Greek music.

Folk clarinets
Besides the members of the immediate clarinet family, closely related instruments can be found in various countries and cultures. The most important thing they have in common is

149

Straight,
metal
contrabass
clarinet

Ab clarinet

Coiled
contra-alto
clarinet

that they all have single reeds. Most of them have only five or six toneholes, and no keys. One of the best known is the wooden Hungarian *tárogató*, which most closely resembles a widely-flared clarinet, or, depending on how you look at it, a wooden soprano saxophone.

WOODWIND INSTRUMENTS

The clarinet belongs to the family of woodwind instruments, as do the saxophone, the flute, the oboe, and the bassoon, among others.

Tipcode CLR-019
In this Tipcode you will hear a alto saxophone, an oboe, a flute, and a bassoon respectively.

TIPCODE

Saxophone
The saxophone is perhaps the instrument that is closest to the clarinet. Both the mouthpiece, with a single beating reed, and the mechanism are very similar.

Conical
One major difference is that saxophones have a brass body that becomes steadily wider from the mouthpiece onwards. This makes it sound and play quite differently. Another major difference is that opening the register key or *octave key* makes the saxophone sound an octave higher.

Flute
If you look only at the keywork, a flute looks a lot like a clarinet

too. This is not surprising: The Boehm clarinet mechanism is derived from the mechanism that Theobald Boehm invented for the flute.

Air stream

The flute has no register key. You move up to a higher register by varying your air stream, a technique known as *overblowing*. When you overblow, you go up an octave.

A soprano saxophone, an alto saxophone, a flute,and an oboe

Oboe

Oboes have a conical body, like saxophones, and they're made of wood, like clarinets. Even so, the oboe sounds very different from both instruments, mainly because it has a different type of reed:

152

An oboe is a *double-reed instrument.* The sound is created by two reeds vibrating against each other, as is the sound of the much larger bassoon.

STOPPED PIPE

Why is the clarinet the only woodwind instrument that goes up a twelfth when you switch to the higher register, rather than an octave, like the other woodwinds? Because it has a (largely) cylindrical tube, which is blocked at one end — by the mouthpiece. As a result, a clarinet acoustically behaves like a *stopped pipe.*

Three times as fast
In a stopped pipe, going up to the next register makes the air vibrate three times as fast. An example: If you play a concert E3, the air vibrates 165 times a second (165Hz). If you then go to the next higher register, the air vibrates three times as fast, at 495Hz, producing a concert B4.

Much lower
Stopped pipes sound a lot lower than you would expect from their length. For instance, a clarinet sounds almost an octave lower than a soprano saxophone, a flute, and an oboe, although all four instruments are pretty much the same length.

Open or conical
In other words, flutes, oboes, and saxophones don't behave like stopped pipes. Flutes don't because they are open at both ends, and saxophones and oboes don't because they have conical instead of cylindrical bores. If you move up to the next register on these instruments, the air starts vibrating twice as fast, which makes the pitch an octave higher.

153

12

How They're Made

Just like many other products, the highest quality clarinets require more hand work and care than lower-budget instruments. But basically, all clarinets are made the same way.

The material for wooden clarinets is delivered to the factory as square-ended blocks or billets: longer ones for the upper and lower joints, short ones for the barrels and big, almost square blocks for the bells. In order to prevent the wood from cracking later, it first needs to be thoroughly dried and cured.

Round
Before the drying process, the square blocks are turned on a lathe to cut them into a round shape, after which a hole is drilled down the middle lengthways. This will later become the bore.

Years or hours
Some companies still leave the wood to dry for a couple of years; others use special kilns that speed up the drying process considerably. More expensive clarinets are often made of older wood, which has the least risk of cracking.

Five stages
After drying, the sections are shaped with a variety of drills and lathes, which are usually computer-controlled. The illustration below shows a lower joint in various stages of manufacture: pre-drilled, roughly turned and dried (1); more finely machined, with rings of wood to accommodate the integral toneholes and tenons (2); showing the chimneys (3); the toneholes and the holes for the mechanism have been drilled (4); lower joint with posts (5).

A lower joint in various stages of manufacture.

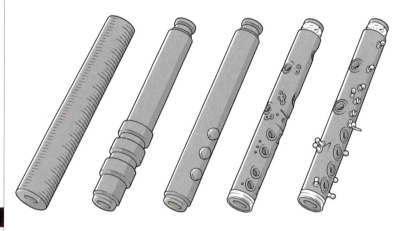

Molds

The sections of plastic clarinets are often molded: The material is poured into a mold, and when it comes out it basically has its final shape.

Polishing

The wooden sections are extensively polished to make them mirror-smooth and shiny. Often they are then submerged in an oil bath for several days or even longer. To make colored instruments, the oil may be mixed with East India ink, for example.

Posts and mechanism

Once all the sections are ready, the posts and rings are attached, and the keywork is mounted and adjusted.

Testing and fine-tuning

Before they leave the factory, instruments are usually play-tested. The more expensive the clarinet, the more attention will usually be devoted to the final testing and adjusting stage. High-end instruments may also be fine-tuned by hand, for example by very carefully reworking the toneholes and the bore.

REEDS AND MOUTHPIECES

Most reeds are made of *Arundo donax*, a type of cane that grows particularly well in Var in southern France, but also in South America, Australia, and elsewhere.

Curing

The plants are harvested when they are two to three years old. By then they have usually grown to about 25 feet (8 meters). After harvesting, the cane is first allowed to dry for a year or more, during which time it cures and develops its golden yellow color.

By size and into shape

The tubes are chopped into short pieces and then sorted by

157

TIPCODE

Tipcode CLR-020
This Tipcode is a visit to a reed company, showing you how reeds are made from start to finish.

size: larger ones for the big reeds used on bass clarinets or large saxophones, smaller ones for small E♭ clarinets, and so on. Afterwards, each tube is usually split into four pieces, the quarters being cut and shaped further by a whole series of machines: The reed is flattened, the facing polished, the profile made and the tip cut into its round shape. At each stage, the reeds are inspected visually, discarding the bad ones.

From cane to reed, showing four of the many steps.

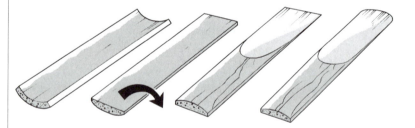

Number
A special device measures the resistance of each reed at the tip. The higher the resistance, the harder the reed, and the higher the number it is given. Next, the reeds are once again inspected thoroughly, stamped, and packed.

Mouthpieces
The production process of a mouthpiece mainly consists of boring, reaming, smoothing, flattening, filing, sanding, buffing, polishing, and related treatments. In a series of steps, the basic hard rubber or plastic mold is worked to exacting specifications, with tolerances of tens of thousandths of an inch — or even

158

less. In most companies a number of operations is undertaken by computer-controlled machines; others still require skilled handwork. The final steps include corking and stamping.

13

Brands

When taking a look at some of the main brand names in the clarinet industry, the French heritage of the instrument is quite clear, with four of the larger companies stemming from that country. That said, clarinets are made all over the world.

There is a relatively small amount of large clarinet companies, i.e., brands that you will come across in most stores that sell woodwind instruments. Some of these companies make instruments in a wide range of prices; others focus on instruments for professionals, or on beginners and step-up instruments. Smaller clarinet makers usually specialize on one or two of those areas as well. Next, there are larger companies that make – typically low-budget – instruments for various companies: The number of brand names exceeds the number of clarinet factories.

Buffer-Crampon is one of the main names in the clarinet world. The French company started when Jean Louis Buffet, whose father already made clarinets, married Zoé Crampon in 1836. One of the founder's uncles co-designed the Boehm clarinet with Hyacinte Klosé (see page 146). Buffet-Crampon also makes oboes, bassoons and saxophones, as well as Besson brasswind instruments.

SINCE 1930 JUPITER.

Jupiter is one of the world's larger woodwind and brasswind instrument brands. All instruments are made by KHS, the Taiwanese parent company that was founded in 1930. The same company also makes Mapex drums.

LeblANC

The history of the Leblanc company goes back to 1750, when flute and oboe maker Denis Noblet started his own company. Around

1900, this family owned company was taken over by Georges Leblanc, whose son Léon started a cooperation with Vito Pascucci in 1946. In 2006, Leblanc became part of the American Conn-Selmer company. Two years later, production was moved to the US. Next to the Leblanc professional and intermediate (Esprit) clarinets, there's a range low lower-budget instruments under the Vito name.

Henri Selmer, solo clarinetist of the Parisian Opéra Comique, started making clarinets in 1885. The French company, that is also known for their large range of saxophones, focuses on intermediate and professional clarinets.

The American Selmer company evolved from the collaboration of Selmer France and the American company Buesscher in the early 1900s. Selmer USA makes student and intermediate clarinets in wood and plastic. The company is not related to Selmer Paris.

The one-man organ factory founded by Torakusu Yamaha in 1889 is now the world's biggest producer of musical instruments, making anything from clarinets to guitars and from synthesizers to pianos. The Japanese company also makes motorbikes, hi-fi equipment, and much more.

163

OTHER COMPANIES

Some other examples of clarinet makers include **Orsi** and **Ripamonti** from Italy, and the Czech company **Amati**, which also produces instruments for other companies, e.g., **Forte**.

US companies

Saxophone maker **Cannonball** markets a series of clarinets under the **Arezzo** name, sporting beginner, intermediate and professional instruments. **Ridenour** is an American company that makes hard rubber clarinets. **Olds** and **E.M. Winston** both produce a small range of student and intermediate clarinets.

Professional instruments

Among the specialists in professional instruments are **Eaton** and **Howarth**, both from the UK, the Italian firm **Patricola**, and the Chilean company **Rossi**, whose products include one-piece B♭ clarinets, and Canadian clarinet maker **Stephen Fox**.

Student instruments

Andino clarinets are related to the professional Rossi instruments. Other lower-priced instruments are made under the names **Barrington** and **Kohlert**, for example. **Palatino** and **Stagg** clarinets are available for less than two hundred dollars.

GERMAN CLARINETS

Most German factories either largely or exclusively make clarinets with the German or Oehler system. A few of the better-known names are **Bernd Moosman**, **Richard Keilwerth**, **Leitner & Kraus**, **Arthur Uebel**, **Püchner**, **Schwenk & Seggelke**, **Schreiber**, and **Hammerschmidt**. The best known German brand name, to be found on very expensive clarinets only, is that of **Herbert Wurlitzer**. The clarinets made by Herbert's father and predecessor Fritz Wurlitzer are at least as celebrated.

BRAND NAMES FROM THE PAST

Some well-known names can be found on older instruments only — but they may very well be used for new instruments some day. Examples include the US names **Bundy** and **Artley**, both brands that focused on student instruments. Two European examples are the French brand **SML** (Strasser-Marigaux-Lemaire), also known as **Marigaux**, which was discontinued in the late 1990s, and **Boosey & Hawkes**, from the UK.

14

Groups and Orchestras

Clarinetists play in concert bands, clarinet choirs, wind quintets, duos, trios, gypsy orchestras, Dixieland groups, jazz bands, symphony orchestras, and all kinds of other groups and ensembles. Here's an introduction to some of those groups, the music they play and what role clarinetists play in them.

The clarinets are of one of the main groups of instruments in a concert band. These large groups, often made up of between about forty and a hundred musicians, may play various styles of music, from classical to modern. The role of the B♭ clarinets can often be compared to that of the violins in a symphony orchestra. Besides a large number of B♭ clarinetists, concert bands also have E♭, alto, and bass clarinetists, and sometimes bigger and smaller clarinets are also used.

Other instruments
Furthermore, a concert band has a brasswind section (trumpet, trombone, and so on), a percussion section, there are other woodwind players (saxes and flutes), and there may be other instruments as well.

Marching bands
A marching band is composed mainly of wind players and percussionists, who perform while marching, either onstage, in parades, or during football games.

Symphony orchestras
The violin usually plays the leading role in the symphony orchestra, as the clarinet often does in concert bands. Most symphony orchestras have two to four clarinetists, just about always on B♭ and A clarinet: Many classical works for symphony orchestras require both instruments. One or two of the clarinetists usually play the E♭ clarinet too, and often there is a separate bass clarinet player. A symphony orchestra also includes other woodwind instruments, a brass section, other strings (viola, cello, double bass), percussion, and other instruments.

Smaller classical ensembles
Classical music can be played in smaller ensembles too, such as chamber orchestras, which have around twenty to forty musicians, or even smaller groups. For example, music has been written for duos (two clarinets), wind trios (clarinet, bassoon, and French horn), wind quartets (plus oboe) and wind quintets (plus flute), sometimes accompanied by a piano, and for all kinds of different line-ups.

168

With strings
Clarinetists often play together with strings. The combined sounds of these instruments blend particularly well. Many composers have written works for clarinet and stringed instruments. Alternatively, as a clarinetist you can replace one of the violinists in a string quartet. That means that you would play with a second violinist, a viola player, and a cellist. Indeed, an alto clarinet could also take over the part of the viola, and a bass clarinetist may replace the cellist.

Solo
Clarinetists can also perform as soloists, just like violinists, pianists, and other musicians. For example, plenty of music has been written for clarinet and orchestra.

Modern classical
Classical music is not just 'old' music, as is often thought. It's still being written today too. Some composers specialize in contemporary or avant-garde music, often using all kinds of unusual sounds and special effects and techniques in their works. The bass clarinet is especially prominent in this type of music, because the instrument offers a lot of scope for experimentation with unusual sounds.

CLARINET CHOIRS

More and more groups are being formed that consist entirely of clarinetists. These clarinet choirs may have five, fifteen, fifty, or even more musicians.

All levels, all styles
Clarinet choirs exist at different levels, from amateur to professional, and may play all kinds of styles: hits, international folk music, works specially written for clarinet choirs, arrangements of works for concert bands and symphony orchestras, and much more besides.

169

From large to small

The bigger a clarinet choir is, the more likely it will be to have a conductor. The B♭ clarinetists are always the biggest group. All kinds of other clarinets may be used in addition, from the tiny A♭ sopranino to the contrabass.

AND MORE

Apart from that, you can play all kinds of other styles as a clarinetist, in a wide variety of groups. Clarinets are used in the folk music of many different countries and regions (the Czech Republic, the Balkans, Turkey and Greece, for example), as they are in gypsy and klezmer orchestras, in world music bands, and in groups that accompany vocalists, choirs, or musicals.

Jazz

No Dixieland band is complete without a clarinetist, and you often find the instrument in big bands too. The saxophone edged out the clarinet in jazz in the 1940s, but in recent years the clarinet has once again been slowly gaining ground, often as a second instrument played by saxophonists.

Jazz and classical

The versatility of the clarinet is shown especially by the many great clarinetists who have become famous by playing jazz while being equally at home playing classical works — from Benny Goodman, Woody Herman, and Eric Dolphy in the past to Eddie Daniels and Don Byron today.

15

Tips on Practicing

Practicing doesn't seem to be every musician's favorite pastime, and that goes for musicians at all levels and ages. Why? Because most musicians want to play their favorite music, rather than spending hours playing scales, etudes, or arpeggios. Because, oftentimes, progress doesn't show right away. And because learning to play an instrument is about long-term gratification, and we seem to have lost touch with that concept. Or because... A number of reasons. But still, it needs to be done — and it can be entertaining, too!

This chapter offers helpful hints on how to practice efficiently, turning practice sessions into rewarding and even inspiring events. Ineffective practice habits are as much work as effective ones, but yield no progress and may cause you to quit playing entirely. Also included in this chapter are helpful tips on where and when to practice, the various components of a good practice session and how to structure it, practice techniques, the importance of memorizing music, and much more.

Sports

Practicing is to music what training is to sports, but there are some major differences. Firstly, most sportsmen train with their teammates, while practicing is something you usually do alone. Secondly, if you play football, soccer, or any other type of sport, you'll probably have a match every week. Most musicians don't have that many opportunities to perform — and usually, being able to perform is why you practice in the first place.

Joining a band

That's why it's important to play in a band, an ensemble, or an orchestra: This offers performance opportunities, it's a great way to meet new friends, and it provides you with clear and realistic goals. Practicing so you can play your part at the next rehearsal is a better motivation than practicing because, well, you're supposed to.

One note

Joining an ensemble is even more important if your play violin, trumpet, flute, clarinet, or any of the other instruments that typically produce one note at a time. These instruments are best suited for group settings, or should at least be accompanied by a piano, for example.

Chords

The piano, keyboards, and guitars are better suited to playing just by yourself, without a band or another form of accompaniment — but even then, playing with other musicians is both fun and inspiring.

Keep on going

It's clear that practice is necessary to achieve a certain level. But should you continue to practice once you've reached a level you're happy with? Maybe not — but if this means that you're limited to playing the same pieces over and over, boredom may set in and the end of your musical endeavors may be near.

No practicing

So can you play without practicing? Of course you can. There are thousands of garage band musicians who never practice; they just play with their friends, and they're having a ball doing so. However, they will usually stop playing once they get a little older, and having no real musical basis, it's unlikely that they'll pick up an instrument again later on in life.

Recreational music making

Participating in a drum circle, for example, allows anyone to play music with a group of people without any prior experience. These and other recreational music-making activities are about socializing, reducing stress, and relaxation more than striving for musical prowess. (Incidentally, that's what most garage bands are about, too.)

Not another obligation

If you want to pursue a career in music, your practice habits should foster diligence, hard work, and making sacrifices (though the latter may not be considered as such). If you don't, practicing should probably be more about fun than about obligations.

Means, goal, or making music?

Some tend to see practice as a goal in and of itself; and the goal is achieved by practicing, say, a half an hour a day. Others consider practice a means to an end — the end usually being the ability to play well (at whatever level) and to perform successfully. You can also consider practice as making music, as a journey that leads to who knows where, and the journey itself is what it's all about.

173

Teachers who make you understand and feel that playing scales is essential will help you enjoy this journey.

How long

One of the most frequently asked questions is, 'How long should I practice?' You could certainly structure your practice sessions to last a required number of minutes per day. But wouldn't it be more interesting to look at what should or could be achieved, so your focus would be on accomplishing a particular task, rather than on filling time? Still, no matter how you look at it, you do need to invest some time in practice, and it's essential to be able to gauge how much time that typically is, so that's what the next section addresses.

The youngest musicians

For very young musicians, things are a bit different. Most experts seem to agree that you can't really speak of 'practicing' until kids are some five or six years of age. For these kids, it's more about spending quality time and having fun with their instrument (if they've actually already chosen one) than about trying to achieve something other than a long-lasting love for music. Playing up to five or ten minutes a day will be fine. The shorter these sessions last and the more fun they are, the more likely a child will want to play three, four, or more days per week.

Six and up

As children get a little older, they'll be able to focus for longer periods, and they'll start to grasp the concept of doing things now that will pay off later. They will also be ready to maintain a practice routine with their teacher's and your guidance. Six- to eight-year-olds should typically spend some fifteen minutes per day on an instrument, say four to six days per week. The older they get, the longer they will be able, and willing, to play.

Half an hour

If you're older — twelve and up — most teachers will probably tell you that playing half an hour a day will help you make sufficient progress to keep things interesting. If you practice effectively, however, you may be able to do your assignments in less time.

174

(This can be so rewarding that you end up playing longer than you intended!)

Short and often

For kids, a practice session lasting a half an hour can be quite long, though, and it may be better to divide the routine up into three ten-minute sessions, or even six sessions of five minutes each. You can do so yourself, too: Short sessions tend to be more effective, with improved retention and more focus.

TIP

Much longer

The better you get, the more you need to practice to progress and maintain your abilities at a desired level. Music majors often practice three to five hours a day. The longer you practice, the sooner you will find that not practicing decreases your musical abilities — so you have to keep up all, or most, of the time!

Music, not minutes

Rather than focusing on a certain amount of time you need to practice, you can look at what should or could be achieved by practicing so you can focus on a set goal (and the music) rather than at the minutes passing by. In order to do so, you must understand exactly what your teacher expects (or you need to be able to set your own goals), and you need to be able to self-assess whether you've achieved those goals.

Assignments

For teachers, this means that they need to be very explicit about their assignments. For example, rather than simply telling you to "learn to play that piece," they must state specific criteria, (_i.e._, "play it with the metronome at 148 beats per minute," or "play a scale five times, without any mistakes, at a certain minimum tempo"). This way, you can simply tell when you've completed the assignment. If the teacher also conveys the practice techniques you need to most effectively reach the goals set for that week, practicing will be much more than a thirty-minute routine to be endured.

175

Your own teacher

Practicing is something that needs to be learned (and often taught). When you practice alone, you're expected to catch your own mistakes, to discover what prompted them, to fix them, and to find a way to prevent them in the future. In effect, when you practice, you are your own teacher. That's not an easy thing to be.

At home

And after all that, when you get to your next lesson or performance, you may find that you're not able to play what you could play at home. Or could you? Did you really hear everything that went wrong? Did you repeat everything to a point where you could even play it under pressure? Probably not — and playing in front of a teacher, your family, or any other type of audience is quite different from playing when there's no one around. This can be practiced too, though. Simply ask your roommate, your kids, friends, or anyone else to come listen to the new piece you have — hopefully — mastered. Getting experienced in playing for others is an important part of the learning process.

When

Ideally, practicing becomes a daily routine, something which is as natural as having dinner, or brushing your teeth. And just like most people have dinner or brush their teeth around the same time every day, practicing is more likely to become a natural part of the day when you do it at or around a set time. Spending time with your instrument on a regular basis may be more important than how much practice you actually do, initially.

Every day?

Should you practice every day? It's unlikely that anything you *have* to do seven days a week will be a lot of fun. That's why many experts will advise you that practicing five to six days will do to make sufficient progress.

Which day?

Sunday often sounds like a good day to skip practicing — but it's also the day of the week that allows for more time to practice, and practicing on Sunday still leaves plenty of time for other activities.

A closer look

If you're having lessons, the day before your lesson is usually the worst one to skip. Also note that it's often very effective to have a short practice session right after your lesson or later that same day. This reinforces the lesson content, and it's a perfect opportunity to take a close look at your weekly assignments.

No time

If it's simply to busy for your intended practice routine, try to sit down and just play one of your favorite pieces, or something else you like to play, rather than not playing at all. Keeping in touch with your instrument is really important.

When?

For many people, it seems best to practice at a set time (such as before school, right after work, before or after dinner). Others prefer to schedule their practice time around other obligations. That way, they can play when they feel like it, rather than having to do so because it happens to be 6:00 PM. Here are some additional tips on planning practice sessions:

- **For students**: Practicing before doing homework provides a nice break between your academic activities, but it may be hard to focus on music if you have lots of homework to do.

- Waiting until **after homework** to practice may feel as if you're never finished; it's like one obligation after the other.

- Planning a practice session **before your favorite TV show** (which is then the reward for practicing) may be more successful than trying to get up and practice when the show is over.

Holidays

It's really important that you keep to your practice sessions during (school) holidays as well. If you don't touch your instrument for a couple of weeks, the first lessons and practice sessions after the holiday may be quite frustrating as you probably won't be able to play those same pieces anymore. You may consider a holiday practice schedule, though.

177

Personal style

People all have their own ways of handling assignments, most likely approaching them the same way they do other things in life. Teachers can help you apply your personal way of handling things to your practice sessions, making them as efficient as possible. Some examples:

- If you're not good at **focusing your attention**, don't start three new pieces at once.

- If you're **afraid to start new pieces**, you may tend to keep on 'practicing' songs you already play very well — so you're dedicating time to practicing, but you're not likely to make any progress.

- If you're **not aware of the mistakes** you make, you will end up rehearsing those mistakes, and it'll be hard to reverse and 'deprogram' those errors. The solution is to learn how to evaluate your own playing before moving on.

WHERE

Ideally, you should be able to practice whenever you feel like it, without being hindered and without hindering others. A practice space needn't be large, just enough to accommodate you and your instrument. If there's room for the instrument to remain unpacked between practice sessions, no valuable time (or inspiration!) gets lost by having to unpack and assemble it before each practice. Ideally, again, you should be able to grab your instrument, tune it if necessary, and play. There are various types of floor-standing and wall-mounted stands on which string instruments, wind instruments, and other small instruments can sit unpacked and out of the way of people, pets, and other potential causes of damage. Special covers are also available to help protect your valuable investments against dust and airborne dirt.

Music stand

If you read sheet music, you will need a music stand. This

affordable piece of hardware promotes good posture (and prevents sore necks), provided it has been set up at the correct height. Nearly all music stands can be folded into a compact size, but it's easier if they can be left standing for the next practice session. This also enhances their life expectancy, as they may be quite flimsy. Do you need to bring a stand to lessons or recitals? Then invest in a second stand that you can take along, leaving the other one at home. Larger type gig bags and instrument cases often have an outer pocket for a music stand.

More on music stands

A basic music stand will set you back less than twenty dollars. *Tip:* Most music stands have two pivoting 'arms' that keep the sheet music in place and prevent music books from flopping closed. If yours doesn't, you can use a rubber band or clothes pins, or you can have your music books spiral-bound so that they stay open. Two more tips:

- Next to black and chrome models, music stands are also available in **bright colors**.

- If you use your music stand at home a lot, consider buying a heavy duty **orchestra model**.

Light

Lighting in the room should be sufficient to see the music easily and clearly. An additional small lamp is usually all that takes. *Tip:* There are special lamps available for music stands specifically.

Stool or chair

A regular stool or chair will usually do. Pianists, keyboard players, drummers, and other musicians are better off using a special (preferably height-adjustable) stool or bench. Without it, posture may be bad and practicing can be tiresome.

Sound systems and computers

Putting up a sound system in your practice area allows you to play along to prerecorded music, play back a recorded lesson, or record your practice sessions. Likewise, a computer can be used to play back CDs, DVDs, and CD-ROMS; to access Internet lessons and

179

music games; or to record practice sessions (if equipped with the right hardware and software). It's also a helpful tool to compose, arrange, transpose, or create music. Synthesizers, home keyboards, and other digital instruments can be hooked up directly to the computer using MIDI, the musical instrument digital interface that is part of all digital music equipment.

And more

There's much more you can do to make practice more effective and fun. Here are some additional tips:

- Consider **lightening up** on practice arrangements if you're very busy. Play your instrument to relax rather then to study.

- Try playing in **another room** of the house from time to time, or even outside, if possible.

- Make sure your practice time is **uninterrupted**, and ask people who call to call back.

- **Varying the structure** of your practice sessions can help keep things fresh. Have your main focus on playing a new piece for a month or so, then address sound production or intonation for a couple of weeks, and so on.

- If you want to practice an hour or more per day, do take one or more **short breaks**. Very brief micro-breaks help you stay focused. If you just can't get that one difficult passage down, comb your hair, pet the cat, eat a carrot, or take a sip of water before trying again. Or try again next week!

- Your instrument should be **in good repair** and tuned properly.

- **Stop if it hurts**. Playing an instrument should not induce pain. If the pain (back, fingers, neck, lips — anywhere) returns every time you practice or play, consult a teacher. The solution could be as simple as getting a different chair or resetting the music stand.

THE COMPONENTS

One of the main keys to effective practice is to have well-structured practice sessions. Depending on your level of playing, the main components of a practice session are:

- Warming up
- Scales and arpeggios
- Etudes
- Sight-reading
- New pieces
- Review

If you're a beginning student, the list will be shorter, and elements will be added as you progress.

Tuning
Most instruments need to be tuned, or the tuning needs to be checked, before you can play. This is where the practice session really begins. As said before, it is easiest if the instrument is always ready to be played — unpacked and assembled. You may want to have valuable and vulnerable instruments covered or packed when they're not being played, however. Also, parts such as strings, and the leather pads on woodwind instruments, tend to last longer if the instrument is covered between practice sessions.

Warming up
Playing music requires a warm up, just like sports do: You may even get injured if you play demanding pieces without a decent warm up. For beginners and intermediate players, the few minutes of 'warming up' are basically meant to get into mood for playing, to get the fingers going, and to get 'into the instrument.' In that sense, it even helps if you take a good long look at your instrument before you play your first notes. Warm-up exercises are not technically demanding; they're the ideal setting for focusing on tone quality, because you can really listen to the sound you're producing.

181

> ### Scales, arpeggios and etudes
> Scales and arpeggios are often used for warm ups, but they're also practiced separately. They're technical exercises that increase your playing proficiency, so your fingers will be able to do what your mind tells them to. Etudes are pieces written with that same goal in mind.

More fun
Many musicians dislike playing scales, etudes, and similar exercise material; it's not as much fun as 'real' pieces, and such exercises often seem meaningless. A good teacher may be able to make you understand why they're so essential, inspiring you to play them with all your heart (though a little less will usually do). Besides, there are various ways to make playing scales and etudes more fun. Some ideas:

- **Focusing on your tone** really helps; imagine what a scale would sound like when played by your all-time favorite musician!.

- Playing scales as if they were **beautiful pieces of music** makes a difference too.

- Make the **volume go up** as you play the scale upwards, and vice versa.

- **Speed up** when playing upwards, and vice versa.

- Speed up and **get louder** one way, and vice versa.

- Play scales in the rhythm of **a song you like**, or play them as triplets.

New pieces
Adding new pieces is necessary to keep progressing, to keep yourself challenged, to expand your repertoire, and to raise your general level of playing. Check pages 187–189 for tips on handling new pieces.

Reviewing repertoire
When you play pieces you already know, there's no struggle,

so you're simply playing music. It's as close to performing as practicing will get — and that's what playing is all about, for most musicians. Reviewing older pieces also keeps your repertoire alive.

Sight-reading

Sight-reading is as essential part of various exams and competitions: You're given a new and unfamiliar piece of music to read and play or sing on demand. It's much the same as reading a story or an article to someone, albeit that playing while reading music is quite a bit harder than reading text aloud. Sight-reading is an important skill for all musicians who want or need to play in situations where they will be expected to perform or rehearse without prior preparation.

And more

A practicing session can consist of lots of other components, such as:

* **Specific exercises** (dynamics, phrasing, improvisation, ear training, extending your range with higher notes, etcetera).

* **Experimenting**: Explore the instrument, try to discover new sounds or playing techniques, try to figure out a melody you've heard, think up new melodies.

* **Playing along** with prerecorded music or special play-along recordings. This is a valid, fun, and effective technique for any musician who doesn't have a band or an orchestra at their disposal. You can also record a performance or rehearsal of the band or orchestra you're in, and use that.

Maintenance

Some instruments require a bit of maintenance at the end of each practice session. Wind instruments have to be disassembled and dried, orchestral string instruments will need the hair of their bows slackened, guitar and bass guitar strings need to be cleaned, and so on. Specific instructions can be found in the relevant chapter of this Tipbook.

TIP

183

Recitals

Have you added a new piece to your repertoire and can you really play it? Again, try playing for friends or housemates. These brief, informal recitals can be very effective. They offer you an opportunity to perform, they may help diminish performance anxiety and they teach you to continue playing through mistakes — and you're most likely to make at least a few of those the first time you play a new piece.

STRUCTURE

To get the most out of your practice sessions, you need to structure them, planning ahead what it is you want to get done.

The beginning and the end

It's usually best to start with things that are relatively easy to play, such as scales. You may also prefer to start each session with a piece you already know. Starting off with an unfamiliar piece can be quite frustrating. Ending the session with a review of familiar repertoire is like a reward for having practiced.

The same order?

You may prefer the safety of doing things in the same order every time; others dislike such routine and rather vary the order of their practice components from day to day.

Two or three sessions

If you divide your practice time into two or more sessions, it's probably most effective to do a little of everything in each session rather then spending the first session only on scales, the second on a new piece, the third on older repertoire, etcetera — but then you might just prefer that.

How much time?

Some experts advise you to dedicate a certain amount of time to each component: a five minute warm-up, ten minutes or etudes, ten on a new piece, and another five to play something familiar. Others will tell you to get rid of the clock, as you want to focus on what you're playing rather than on the minutes passing by.

Goals

The clearer your musical goals are, the easier it will be to practice effectively. When defining these goals, it often helps to distinguish:

- **long-term goals**: I'd like to join such-and-such band, or play a solo recital by the end of the year or this month.

- **mid-term goals**: I'd like to finish this method book, or be able to play these pieces.

- and **short-term goals**, which may differ for each practice session: I'd like to memorize this piece, or play that section ten times without a mistake.

PRACTICING TECHNIQUES

Practicing efficiently is also a matter of applying the right practicing techniques. Improving your tone requires a different technique than increasing your speed, or tackling a new piece.

Small jobs

One of the best ways to make your practice session more effective and fun is to break down large jobs into a number of small jobs. Rather than tackling a new piece from beginning to end, break it down into four or eight measures to be played per day, for example. This way, you can have a small success every day, rather than fighting to master the entire piece in one week.

Revision

If a new piece is broken up into sections comprised of a number of bars, reviewing the sections that were done on previous days should be an essential part of each practice session. Learning an instrument is most effectively done through frequent repetition.

185

(In various languages, the word for 'practice' literally means repetition!)

The right notes

Repetition results in long-term memory storage, which is good. The problem, however, is that your memory does not select what should be stored and what should not. If you consistently repeat an incorrect passage, that's what will be stored, and if you play the wrong note half of the time, there's a fifty-fifty chance that the wrong note will come out at your performance. So when repeating things, make sure you play the right notes — and slow down as much as you need on order to do so.

Five or ten

Some teachers may advise you to move to the next section only when you're able to play the current section correctly five (or ten) times in a row. If you make a mistake, you start counting all over again — until you get all five (or ten) correct. Others may not be concerned with the number of repetitions, so long as you play it right the final time: This way, your fingers are supposed to 'remember' the right moves.

Slow down

A difficult passage may be hard to play correctly, and playing it right five times in a row may seem impossible. The solution, again, is to slow things down. Slow, in this case, means really slow. Take one, two, or more seconds for every note, and disregard note values for now. Take a metronome, set it at sixty BPM (*i.e.*, sixty Beats Per Minute, equaling one beat per second), and let it tick one, two, or more times before moving on to the next note. Such

TIP

> ### Tone
>
> *For advanced players, practicing a piece really slowly is also a good way to work on their tone, and to get the smallest nuances of a piece right: dynamics, intonation, phrasing, and everything else beyond hitting the right notes at the right time.*

slow tempos make you aware of the movements your fingers have to make to get from note to note, or from chord to chord.

A NEW PIECE

There are also various practicing techniques for handling new pieces. As mentioned before, a piece can be divided up into four bar, eight bar, or longer sections, revising the previous sections (and playing them absolutely correctly) before moving on. This is just one of many approaches, and all of these approaches can be mixed to come up with a combination that is most effective for you.

Challenge

Starting a new piece is a positive challenge to some, while it makes others feel as if they have to start all over again. Of course, avoiding new pieces will yield no progress. Also, learning to tackle new pieces can help you tackle other problems and deal with new, complex subjects as well — which is just one of the reasons that music students perform better in various academic fields. Some of the tips below apply to more advanced musicians only; others work for beginners too.

Listen

As said before, it is essential that you practice a piece playing only the correct notes. It helps if you can first listen to a recorded version of the new piece so you know what it's supposed to sound like before attempting to play it. Of course, you can also ask your teacher to play the piece for you.

Read along

Reading along while listening to a new piece helps you link the notes to the music. With complex pieces, study the part visually before listening to it, so you won't be surprised by repeats and other markings. Reading the music before playing it also gives you the opportunity to check out all dynamic signs and tempo markings, to locate accidentals (flats, sharps, naturals), and

187

numerous other details and characteristics of the piece — and you don't have to worry about playing the instrument at the same time you're reading.

More

If you have a teacher, ask him or her to tell you about the new piece of music: its general character, its form (12-bar blues or 32-bar AABA? Rondo or suite?), the style, the composer, the era in which it was written, and so on. After all, there's more to music than simply executing the composer's notes.

Step by step

Beginning players are often advised to approach a new piece step by step. First, clap the rhythm of the notes, counting aloud as you go. When you've got the rhythm down, play the melody without paying attention to the rhythm. Once you can clap the rhythm and play the right notes, combine the two — very, very slowly. This approach works well for advanced players too. Pianists and other keyboard players can practice the left hand part first, and then the right hand, before attempting to play a new piece with both hands.

The trouble spots

Alternatively, depending on your ability and the complexity of the piece, you can play the piece through at an easy tempo, spotting the difficult bits as you go. Playing a piece as such, with mistakes and all, may give you a general idea of what it is about (assuming you haven't heard it before). Other players rather start by locating the tricky bits and figure them out first. A tip: If you're working on a tricky section, always include a few notes or bars before and after that particular section in order to make the tricky section a part of the whole thing, rather than an isolated hurdle that might scare you off every time you see it coming.

Analyzing the trouble spots

If you're having a problem with a certain section, you can simply play it again and again (and again) until you get it right. However, it might be more effective to find out what's causing the problem in the first place. Is it the fingering (which fingers to use for which note)? The rhythm? Or can you not play the part with your left hand while your right hand is doing something else? Or is it a note higher or lower than you can play or sing? Without proper answers to those questions, it will be hard to move on — and before you get to the answers, you need to come up with the right questions. Again, this is something a teacher may be able to help you with. One step beyond analyzing the trouble spots is developing exercises that help the student tackle them. This is something advanced players do for themselves, and something that teachers should teach their students.

MEMORIZING MUSIC

Opinions differ as to whether you should memorize music. Some teachers insist that you should; others feel that memorizing music should be optional, unless you're considering a professional career in music.

Why?
Why would you learn to memorize a piece that can simply read?

- It can help make you **a better musician**. If you don't have to focus on reading, you can fully focus on other elements — tone, phrasing, dynamics, and so on — and listen to yourself play. Also, to play from memory you have to really know a piece inside out, which can only help improve your performance.

- It makes you **look good**. Professional soloists play without sheet music, so why can't you?

- On some instruments, playing by heart allows you **to watch your hands** as you play. Not a very professional approach, but it can be handy.

Why not?
Of course, there's no need to keep musicians from memorizing music (and some are extremely good at it), but why force them?

- Being required to play without sheet music makes a

performance **an even more** stressful event — and wasn't making music about enjoying yourself?

- Worrying about what'll happen if you **forget the piece** does not inspire a good performance. It takes away more energy from the music than reading notes does. In other words, some just need sheet music to play well, even while others might play better without it.

- If you're **not good at memorizing** music, learning pieces by heart may take up valuable time that's probably better spent on things you can do to grow musically. Do note that learning to memorize music takes time too: It's not something you just can do.

Techniques and tips

There are various ways and techniques to memorize music. What works great for you, may not work for your friend, and vice versa. The following shortlist helps you recognize how typically handle things, and offers some suggestions.

- You can memorize a piece **as you learn it**, or you can wait to memorize it once you can play it correctly.

- Memorize **small sections** at a time. For some, a small section is one or two bars; for others, it's half a page. Start with the first section, and add subsequent sections only after you've mastered previous sections.

- Some memorize the **difficult parts first**, repeating them so often that they become as easy to play as the rest of the piece. Only after mastering the difficult parts do they include the other sections. *Tip:* Many teachers claim that you should never play a piece in any other order than the one intended.

- Most musicians memorize a piece from beginning to the end, but there are those who prefer to do it **the other way around**, working their way back to the beginning.

- You can also memorize bits and pieces **as you go**. Try not to look at the music while you're playing, glancing up only as you feel you need to. Bit by bit, over time, you will learn to play the entire piece by heart.

- If you **repeat a piece** or a section over and over, you're using your finger memory or tactile memory. Your fingers know what to do because they've been trained to execute the patterns that are required for that piece of music. It's a relatively easy way to memorize, but it's not very reliable. Changing the tempo of the piece may confuse you (or your fingers). If you want to know if you've really memorized the music, play it at an extremely slow tempo and see what happens.

- Alternatively, you can analyze the piece **step by step**, studying every single aspect of it. This requires a lot of knowledge (scales, harmony, etcetera), but it's the most reliable way to memorize.

- Practicing a piece **away from your instrument** may help you memorize it. Just play it in your imagination, first with, then without the music. This is referred to as shadow practicing or armchair memorizing. You can also try to hear the piece in your head without playing it, before you go to sleep, or on your way to work. Or sing it while you're taking a shower.

- It also helps if you make up **a story that fits the music**!

- **Slow practicing** is good for memorizing music.

- And when you're almost done, **put the book away**. Don't leave it on the music stand, pretending or trying not to peek, but put it in the other room. Out of sight, out of mind? Then try again.

16

Being Prepared

A dry throat, butterflies in your stomach, jitters and shakes, weak knees, trembling fingers, a throbbing heart... All familiar sensations to anyone who ever took a music exam or climbed a stage to perform or audition. And those who claim they've never experienced such symptoms are probably lying.

Nervousness and performing go hand in hand. It's a sign that you're undergoing an adrenaline rush, and without it, performances may be less exciting for both the players and the audience. But stage fright can get so bad that it causes you to fail an audition, not make the grade, or mess up your performance. This chapter shares some ideas on reducing audition anxiety, stage fright, and exam nerves.

Books

Many books have been written on this subject, and there is a whole lot more to be said and taught about it. The tips in this chapter touch the mere basics; and as obvious as they seem, they're often quite effective.

Adults and kids

Kids seem to suffer less from jitters and other anxiety symptoms than most teens and adults. So one of the best ways to prevent such feelings in the first place is to begin performing in public at an early age, be it with a school band, playing mini-recitals for the family every week or after each practice session — even if it's only briefly. As taking this advice may not be an option if you're already beyond early childhood, keep on reading.

PREPARING YOURSELF

First, a look at what could, or should, be done beforehand.

Practice, practice, practice

If you're not fully prepared for a performance, an audition, or a music exam, you have every reason to be nervous. Practicing efficiently, possibly under the guidance of a teacher, is one key to abating performance anxiety. A tip: The closer the time of the main event comes, the more important it is to focus practice sessions on problem areas, rather than on playing known material. A rule of thumb is to be able to play the tricky bits at least five to ten times in a row without stumbling. Only then can you be sure that you've got them down. *Tip:* Make yourself start over from the beginning after each mistake, even if it's the very last note. This can make playing the final run almost as thrilling as an audition.

> **Too late**
>
> *If you feel that you have to spend hours practicing the day before the performance, or on the actual day, you probably failed to use your previous practice sessions to the fullest.*

TIP

Slips

Even professionals make mistakes, so preparing a piece includes preparing for stumbles and slips. Practice how to recover quickly and continue to play in the correct tempo. You can learn how to deal with slip-ups. One simple tip: do not make a face as this will just draw everyone's attention to your mistake. Note that there are music teachers who specialize in audition preparation!

Memory

You may play from memory to impress the jury or the members of the band, but consider bringing your sheet music along if memorization was not required. Having it there will make it easier to start over if you do slip. Does your piece require page turning? Then it would be helpful to memorize the first section on the following page. Another tip for auditions or exams: Make sure you make a list of the pieces you're going to play and bring it with you. It really doesn't look good if you've forgotten the title of your next piece.

Accompanist

If you're going to play with an accompanist during the performance, it's best if that's the person you rehearse with as well. Playing with a stranger can cause added tension, and a familiar face can be a great confidence booster. Even if not required, you may want to consider doing your piece with accompaniment (if you're not already the pianist or guitarist): Having another person there may help reduce stress, and it usually makes for a more entertaining performance too.

195

Deal with it

No matter how well-prepared you are, exams, auditions, and performances will induce stress and nervousness. Dealing with this is part of the learning process of playing, period. Practice doesn't make perfect, but the more you play (and the more exams or auditions you do), the better you will eventually become at handling stage fright.

Surrender

Fighting your nerves is not a good idea either. Doing so can even add to your stress level, which is probably already substantial. Telling yourself to be calm usually doesn't work either. You aren't calm, so it's actually better to just surrender to that. The fact that your nerves can make your performance less than brilliant just shows how important it is to be well-prepared.

Mock auditions

The more used to playing for an audience you are, the less likely you are to be nervous for auditions or exams. Still, these situations are different from regular performances: They occur less frequently and there's usually a lot riding on them. A mistake made during a performance typically has fewer consequences than a slip at an audition. Staging mock auditions (a.k.a. placebo auditions or dress rehearsals) often helps in getting used to the extra tension. They can take place at home, while playing for family and friends. Some teachers organize mock auditions too. *Tip:* Turn mock auditions into a complete performance, including a formal entrance into the room, presenting yourself, and so on. Also, ask your audience to evaluate your playing afterwards to ensure that they were attentive to every note you played. Scary? That's the idea.

Recording in advance

Recording the pieces you'll be playing at the audition or exam can by very effective. First, a recording allows you to listen and evaluate your performance, as it's very difficult to do that while you're playing. And the recorded results can give you the objectivity you need to really assess what you're doing. Second, a simple recording device can have the same effect as an attentive audience in that it can make you nervous enough to perhaps make the kind of mistakes you would in front of a real audience. Getting used to the presence of a recording device is quite similar to getting used to an audience, so that makes it effective training.

Evaluate the recording

Don't forget to evaluate the recording, and don't listen for mistakes only. Pay close attention to timing, intonation, dynamics, and all other elements that make for a great performance, including tone. Evaluating the latter requires good recording and playback equipment. *Tip:* First warm up, and then try to play your prepared pieces and scales right during the first take — just like in real life!

Presentation

Are you required or do you want to dress a certain way for the performance? Then decide beforehand what you're going to wear, how to wear your hair, etcetera. Don't wait until the day of the show to do this, but get your look together at least the day before.

Sleep

And don't forget: A good night's sleep, or a nap before an afternoon performance, often works wonders!

SHOW TIME

There are many remedies for reducing nerves on the day of your performance too. First of all, leave home early so there's no need to rush, and make sure there's plenty of time to prepare for the performance once you're on site.

Relax

For some, simply repeating the words, 'I'm calm, I'm cool,' is enough to help them relax, but most people need more than this. There are many different techniques, ranging from deep-breathing exercises to meditation, yoga, or special methods like the Alexander Technique or neurofeedback. You may also benefit from simple stretching, jumping, and other physical movement, and for some, screaming helps.

Transfer your stress
Another idea is to find a physical release for your stress. For example, take a paperclip along and hold it when you feel nervous, imagining that all of your extra energy is being drawn through your hand into the paperclip — then throw it away before you go onstage.

Warming-up
Warm-up routines (long notes, scales, and so on) not only get you musically prepared to perform, they can also help you relax. Long, slow notes are more effective than up-tempo riffs, obviously. If you feel the need to go through your scales and prepared pieces once more, you probably aren't really ready. *Tip:* Find a quiet place to prepare, if possible.

Silence
If there's no opportunity to actually play before you go onstage, just moving your fingers over the keys or the strings of your instrument will help. Wind instrument players can warm up their instrument by blowing warm air through it.

The instrument
Make sure the instrument is in good repair, and thoroughly check it before the performance. Exam judges may forgive a broken string, a failed reed, or a stuck valve, but even so, these things won't promote a confident performance. Brasswind players: If you've warmed up to prepare for your performance, make sure to drain your horn before going onstage.

Tuning and warming-up
Tuning the instrument under the observant eyes of your audience, the jurors, or the examiners may be nerve-wracking, so make sure you take care of this in advance, if possible.

198

Imagine

Many musicians fight their nerves by conjuring calming imagery. They imagine playing at home or on their favorite stage rather than in front of a jury; or they concentrate on a recent holiday, or pretend they're on a deserted island. Others promise themselves that this is their very last performance ever, so they need to give it all — now or never.

Pep talk

Giving yourself a pep talk may help too. But rather than just telling yourself to be cool and calm, tell yourself that you wouldn't even be here if your teacher hadn't thought you were ready — you've earned your way there.

Focus

Don't focus on the outcome of the audition or exam. Instead, concentrate on your music, as that's really what it's all about. What may also help is to make your objective the demonstration of the beauty of the music you're going to play, rather than how impressive a player you are.

Smile

Smile when you enter the room. It will make you both look and feel better. Stand up straight and put both feet firmly on the floor. It helps, really.

A different type of audience

Auditioners and examiners are a particular kind of audience. They're there to judge your playing, rather than just enjoy the music. Still, it's good to realize that they're there for you; know that they want you to play your best and to make you feel at ease.

Any audience

It may help to calm you if you look at your examiners and auditioners the same way you'd look at a 'regular' audience: Tell yourself that they're all very kind people (which they usually are, so this shouldn't be too hard). Make eye contact with your jurors just as you would any other audience, and smile. And just as you might focus on the people you know, or the ones responding

199

favorably to you in a regular performance, focus on the juror who smiles back at you.

> ## Imagine
>
> *Another approach is to completely ignore the audience (imagine that you're playing at home alone); but realize that this might not work at an audition or an exam. A popular method is to image the audience (large or small, jurors or not) sitting in their underwear, feeling even more uncomfortable than you are onstage. Or think of the audience as non-musicians who will be impressed by every single note you play, or as the ultimate experts who showed up just to hear you play!*

The first note

Take a couple of seconds before you start playing. Breathe. Get the tempo of the piece going in your head, or even sing the first few bars in your mind; imagine yourself playing the song. Then it's time for the first note. Make it sound great, and enjoy your performance!

AND MORE

If none of the above works for you, try consulting one of the many books on the subject. Another option is to take a yoga or meditation course, for example, or consider a drama class.

Food and drinks

Various types of food and drink are said to make anxiety worse (e.g., coffee, tea, and other products with caffeine, sugar, or salt), while others help to soothe your nerves. Bananas contain potassium, which helps you relax, and there are various types of calming herbal teas, for example. Alcohol may make you feel more relaxed, but it definitely inhibits motor skills, judgment, and clarity — so avoid drinking alcoholic beverages.

Drugs

Many professional musicians take beta blockers (heart medication, actually) to combat their performance anxiety. This type of drug is considered relatively safe, and it works a lot faster than a yoga course and most other relaxation techniques. But you should wonder if music is your thing if you need drugs to do it, even if it's only for high-stress situations, like an audition. Try instead to reduce, if not eliminate, stressors; only do things that make you feel good, and avoid those that induce anxiety. Music is supposed to be fun!

Chapter 15 and 16 were taken from Tipbook Music for Kids and Teens *(see page 237) and adapted for* Tipbook Clarinet.

Tipcode List

The Tipcodes in this book offer easy access to short videos, sound files, and other additional information at www.tipbook.com. For your convenience, the Tipcodes in this Tipbook have been listed below.

Tipcode	Topic	Chapter	Page
CLR-001	Fingers on the keys	2	7
CLR-002	The register key	2	11
CLR-003	Three registers	2	14
CLR-004	Ranges of four clarinets	2	19
CLR-005	A-concert pitch (440Hz)	5, 8	54, 122
CLR-006	Difference between 440 and 442Hz	5	55
CLR-007	'Problem notes'	5	77
CLR-008	Play on keys	5	79
CLR-009	German mouthpiece with cord	6	85
CLR-010	Adjusting underside reed	7	109
CLR-011	Cutting a reed	7	109
CLR-012	Using Dutch rush	7	110
CLR-013	Assembling a clarinet	8	117
CLR-014	Opening the bridge	8	118
CLR-015	Reed on mouthpiece	8	120
CLR-016	Tuning fork	8	122
CLR-017	Swab	8	126
CLR-018	Cleaning a pad	8	129
CLR-019	Sax, flute, oboe, and bassoon	11	151
CLR-020	Making reeds	12	158

Glossary

This glossary briefly explains most of the jargon touched on so far. It also contains some terms that haven't been mentioned yet, but which you may come across in other books, in magazines, or online. Most terms are explained in more detail as they are introduced in this book. Please consult the index on pages 232–234.

12th key

If you open the *12th key* or *register key* of a clarinet, the note you are playing goes up by a twelfth, taking you to the next register. See also: *Register, register key.*

17/6

Most clarinets have seventeen keys and six rings.

A clarinet

Sounds a half step lower than the B♭ clarinet.

Acute register

See: *Register, register key.*

Albert clarinet

See: *German clarinet.*

Altissimo register

See: *Register, register key.*

Alto clarinet

The alto clarinet is slightly larger than a B♭ clarinet. It's an E♭ instrument, sounding an octave lower than a soprano E♭ clarinet.

Articulated G♯

Extra key that makes various trills easier to play.

Auxiliary E♭ lever

An extra lever that allows you to operate the A♭/E♭ key with your left little finger, as well as with the right one.

Baffle

A baffle lowers the palate of the mouthpiece, making the sound brighter and more direct.

Barrel

The joint that connects the mouthpiece and the upper joint. Also known as *tuning barrel* and *socket.*

Bass clarinet

Sounds an octave lower than a soprano clarinet in B♭.

Bell

The widely flared end of the clarinet. The larger clarinets (e.g., the alto and the bass clarinet) have a metal bell.

B♭ clarinet

The most popular clarinet is the soprano clarinet in B♭: the C fingering sounds a concert B♭.

Boehm clarinet

The Boehm clarinet or French clarinet is the most popular type of clarinet. See also: *German clarinet.*

Bore

The dimensions and shape of the inside of the instrument. Most important 'component' of the clarinet, along with the bore of the mouthpiece (67–68) and the barrel (72).

Break register

See: *Register, register key.*

Bridge

The connection between the upper joint and the lower joint. Also called *bridge mechanism* or *connection*, or *correspondence.*

Chalumeau

1. See: *Register, register key.* 2. Forefather of the clarinet.

Chamber
The internal space of a mouthpiece.

Clarinet register, clarino register, clarion register
See: *Register, register key.*

Closed-hole keys
Keys with solid key cups and a pad, as opposed to ring keys. Also known as *plateau-style keys.*

Concert pitch
See: *Transposing instruments.*

Connection
See: *Bridge.*

Dalbergia melanoxylon
See: *Grenadilla.*

Double cut
See: *French file cut.*

E♭ clarinet
A smaller clarinet that sounds a fourth higher than the regular B♭ clarinet.

Embouchure
The way you use your lips, jaws, tongue, and all the muscles around them when playing a wind instrument.

Facing
1. Used to indicate the tip opening of a mouthpiece, for the lay (curvature, length) or both. See also: *Lay.*
2. The underside of a reed.

File cut
See: *French file cut.*

Forked B♭
An extra (seventh) ring, offering an alternative (fork) fingering for B♭.

French clarinet
Another name for the Boehm clarinet. See: *Boehm clarinet.*

French file cut
A reed with a *French file cut* has an extra section at the end of the thick part filed away in a straight line. Also known as *file cut* or *double cut*, as opposed to reeds with a *single cut.*

Full Boehm
A rare type of clarinet with many extra keys and options.

German clarinet
German clarinets have a different bore and a different mechanism, mouthpiece, and reed than French or Boehm clarinets. There are various systems, such as the German or Albert system, and the Oehler system.

Grenadilla
The most commonly used type of wood for clarinets. Also known as ebony, m'pingo or African blackwood, and officially called *Dalbergia melanoxylon.*

Integral toneholes
See: *Toneholes.*

Intonation
The better the intonation of a clarinet is, the easier it is to play in tune.

Key cups
The actual 'lids' that stop the toneholes. Also known as *pad cups.*

205

Key opening
See: *Venting.*

Keys
Clarinets have (*plateau-style, closed hole* or *covered*) keys with pads, and open rings or ring keys.

Keywork
See: *Mechanism.*

Klosé clarinet
Another name for the French or Boehm clarinet, invented by Hyacinte Klosé.

Lay
The area where the mouthpiece curves away from the reed, from the tip of the reed to the point where the reed touches the mouthpiece. See also: *Facing, facing length.*

Ligature
A clamp that attaches your reed to your mouthpiece.

Long-pipe notes, long-tube notes
The notes you play with most or all of the keys closed, so that you are using a long section of the clarinet tube. When all or most of the keys are open, you play *short-pipe notes* or *short-tube notes.*

Lyre
Holder for sheet music, to be mounted onto the instrument.

M'pingo
See: *Grenadilla.*

Mechanism
The entire system of keys and rods that allow you to open and close all the toneholes. Also called the *keywork* or *key system.*

Mode
See: *Register, register key.*

Mouthpiece
How you sound and play depends primarily on your mouthpiece and your reed.

Mouthpiece cushion
Self-adhesive pad that protects both the mouthpiece and your teeth.

Neck
Alto, bass, and other large clarinets have a metal neck instead of a barrel. Also known as *crook.*

Octave key
See: *Register key.*

Oehler clarinet
See: *German clarinet.*

Pad cups
See: *Key cups.*

Pads
Small discs made of felt or cork, covered in animal membrane, leather, or plastic, which seal the toneholes.

Plateau-style keys
See: *Closed-hole keys.*

Posts
The metal pillars by which the mechanism is attached to the clarinet.

Power-forged keys
Keys that are shaped by pressure, rather than cast.

Rails
The tip rail and the side rails are the three edges of the window of a mouthpiece.

Reed
The sound source of the instrument. Precisely shaped piece of cane, attached to the mouthpiece.

Reed cutter
Tool used to slightly shorten reeds that are too light.

Reed guard
Protective holder for reeds.

Reform Boehm clarinet
Reform Boehm clarinets have a German bore and a French mechanism. See also: *Boehm clarinet.*

Register, register key
The register key allows you to move from the low *chalumeau register* to the *clarinet register* (also known as *clarion register, clarino register, upper register* or *overblown register*). The third and highest register is called the *acute register,* the *altissimo register,* or the *aigu register.* The register key is also known as the *speaker key, 12th key* or, wrongly, the *octave key.* The four highest notes of the chalumeau register (G–B♭) are indicated as the *break* or *throat register.* The registers are also referred to as *modes.*

Register tube
Small tube in the register key tonehole; also known as *speaker tube.*

Rings, ring keys
See: *Keys.*

Short-pipe notes, short-tube notes
See: *Long-pipe notes, long-tube notes.*

Single cut
See: *French file cut.*

Single-reed instruments
Like saxophones, clarinets use a mouthpiece with a single reed. The oboe and the bassoon are examples of double-reed instruments.

Socket
See: *Barrel.*

Soprano clarinet
The most popular clarinet is the soprano clarinet in B♭. There are other soprano clarinets in A, C, D and E♭.

Speaker key
See: *Register, register key.*

Speaker tube
See: *Register tube.*

Stopped pipe
A cylindrical instrument which is blocked at one end acoustically behaves like a stopped pipe. The clarinet belongs to this group.

Throat register
See: *Register, register key.*

207

Thumb key
See: *Register, register key.*

Thumb rest
Helps support the instrument.

Tip opening
The distance between the tip of your reed and the tip of your mouthpiece. See also: *Facing, facing length.*

Toneholes
The toneholes in your clarinet allow you to play different pitches. They are often undercut, which means that each hole gets slightly larger toward the bottom. Integral toneholes are explained on page 52.

Transposing instruments
On a transposing instrument, the note that sounds (concert pitch) is different from the one you finger. A fingered C on a B♭ clarinet sounds an B♭ concert pitch. A fingered C on an alto clarinet sounds an E♭. Non-transposing instruments (the piano, the concert flute, or the C clarinet, for example) play in *concert pitch.*

Trill keys
Only the upper two of the four keys that you play with the side of your right hand index finger are actually designed for playing trills, but often all of them are referred to as *trill keys.*

Tuning
You tune a clarinet by pulling two or more joints apart slightly, or by using a different tuning barrel.

Tuning barrel
See: *Barrel.*

Tuning ratios
The pitch differences between notes played with, or without the register key (E/B, F/C, and so on).

Tuning rings
Thin rings designed to fill up the groove that is formed inside the tube when tuning a clarinet.

Undercut toneholes
See: *Toneholes.*

Upper register
See: *Register, register key.*

Venting
Exactly how far the closed keys open when you press them affects the sound of your clarinet, but also its intonation. Also called *key opening.*

Window
The opening of the mouthpiece.

Want to Know More?

Tipbooks supply you with basic information on the instrument of your choice, and everything that comes with it. Of course there's a lot more to be found on all of the subjects you came across on these pages. This section offers a selection of magazines, books, helpful websites, and more.

MAGAZINES

Some examples of magazines that offer plenty of information on clarinets and clarinet playing are:

- *The Clarinet* (US): International Clarinet Association, www.clarinet.org

- *Windplayer* (US): www.windplayer.com

- *Australian Clarinet & Saxophone:* www.clarinet-saxophone.asn.au

- *Clarinet & Saxophone* (UK): www.cassgb.org

BOOKS

Countless books have been written about clarinets and clarinetists. Those listed below cover the instrument itself and discuss other subjects, such as technique, history, and repertoire, at greater length.

- *Clarinet*, Jack Brymer, Yehudi Menuhin Music Guides (Kahn & Averill, Engeland, 2006; 296 pages; ISBN 978-1871082128).

- *Cambridge Companion to the Clarinet*, Colin Lawson (Cambridge University Press, 2008; 260 pages; ISBN 978-0521476683).

- *The Clarinet and Clarinet Playing*, David Pino (Dover Publication, New York, 1998; 320 pages; ISBN 978-0486402703).

- *Clarinet Acoustics*, O. Lee Gibson (Indiana University Press, 1994/1998; 84 pages; ISBN 0253211727).

- No longer in print, but still to be found in libraries are *The Clarinet; Some Notes on Its History & Construction*, F. Geoffrey Rendall; edition revised by Philip Bate (Ernest Benn Ltd., London, 1971; 206 pages; ISBN 0510-36701-1), and the four volumes of *The Complete Clarinet Player* by Paul Harvey.

REEDS

For making and adjusting reeds, you may want to check out the following publications:

- *Making Clarinet Reeds by Hand*, Walter Grabner (www.clarinetXpress.com).

- *Perfect a Reed … and Beyond*, Ben Armato (1996; 43 pages; www.reed-wizard.woodwind.org).

- *A Book for the Clarinet Reed-Maker*, Ronald V. Vazquez (1993; 90 pages).

- *Handbook for Making and Adjusting Single Reeds*, Kalmen Opperman (44 pages).

- *The Single Reed Adjustment Manual*, Fred Ormand (Amilcare Publications, 2000; 84 pages).

- *Selection, Adjustment, and Care of Single Reeds*, Larry Guy (Rivernote Press, SB, 57 pages).

- *Working the Single Reed*, David Bourque (DVD; BCL Enterprises, 2005).

Do note that most of these publications are not available in regular book stores.

CLARINET ASSOCIATIONS

Various clarinet associations organize meetings, seminars, workshops, festivals, and other activities for clarinetists, next to publishing a magazine or journal (see page 178). Some examples are listed below.

- International Clarinet Association: www.clarinet.org

- Clarinet & Saxophone Society of Great Britain: www.cassgb.org

- Australian Clarinet & Saxophone: www.clarinet-saxophone.asn.au

WEBSITES

There is a lot of clarinet information available online. Do check out the websites of clarinet and reed makers, mouthpiece and barrel specialists and other manufacturers, as well as non-commercial websites such as:

- The Clarinet Pages: www.woodwind.org/clarinet

- World Clarinet Alliance: www.wka-clarinet.org

211

- Clarinet Zone: www.clarinetzone.i12.com

- Sherman Friedland's Clarinet Corner: clarinetcorner.wordpress. com

- The Clarinet and Saxophone Society of Great Britain: www. cassgb.org

- Jazz-clarinet.com: www.jazz-clarinet.com

LOOKING FOR A TEACHER

You can also look for a teacher online. Simply search for "clarinet teacher" and the name of area or city where you live, for example, or visit one of the following special interest websites:

- PrivateLessons.com: www.privatelessons.com

- MusicStaff.com: www.musicstaff.com

- The Music Teachers List: www.teachlist.com

- The Tutor Pages (UK): www.thetutorpages.com

Fingering Charts

On the following pages, you'll find the basic fingering charts for the B♭ clarinet, as well as a number of practical alternate fingerings. An interactive variation on this chapter can be found at www.tipbook.com.

This section provides you with the basic fingerings for each tone of the entire range of the B♭ clarinet, as well as with a selected variety of *alternate* or *false fingerings*.

Registers

The range of the clarinet is usually subdivided in the following three registers:

- the **chalumeau register**: E3 to B♭4

- the **clarinet register**: B4 to C5

- the **high register**: C♯5 to C7

The three registers of the B♭ clarinet.

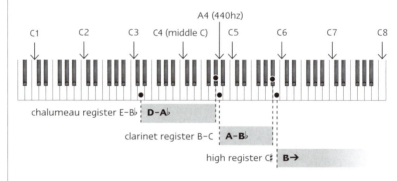

Alternate fingerings

Many notes can also be played using one or more alternate fingerings or false fingerings.
Alternate fingerings are used for three purposes.

- They can make **technical passages** easier to play.

- They can be used to adjust the **pitch** of certain tones.

- They can be used to alter the **timbre** of a tone.

Note that the the difference between regular or basic and alternate fingerings is arbitrary; what some teachers or clarinet schools consider basic fingerings, others think of as alternate fingerings.

Some do, some don't

Do note that some alternate fingerings may work great on one instrument, but sound flat, sharp, harsh or dull on another clarinet. The quality of the instrument and the mouthpiece may be influential here.

There's more

There are many more useful and musical alternate fingerings for clarinet players in all styles. You can find them both in dedicated books and online. Check for examples by searching for 'clarinet fingering charts'.

Final tip

These Tipbook fingering charts were selected by clarinetist, bass clarinetist, and teacher, Jelte Althuis. He'd like to share one final tip with you: When playing the high register of your instrument, you may adjust the timbre and the intonation of various pitches by trying out various fingerings. First of all, see what happens if you close any one of your four right-hand little finger keys!

215

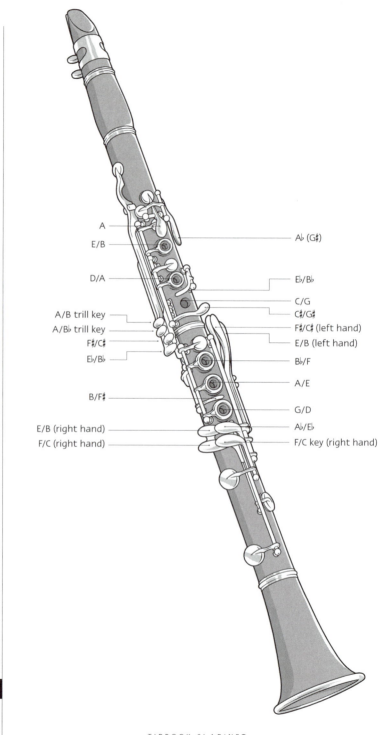

A

E/B

D/A

A/B trill key

A/B♭ trill key

F♯/C♯

E♭/B♭

B/F♯

E/B (right hand)

F/C (right hand)

A♭ (G♯)

E♭/B♭

C/G

C♯/G♯

F♯/C♯ (left hand)

E/B (left hand)

B♭/F

A/E

G/D

A♭/E♭

F/C key (right hand)

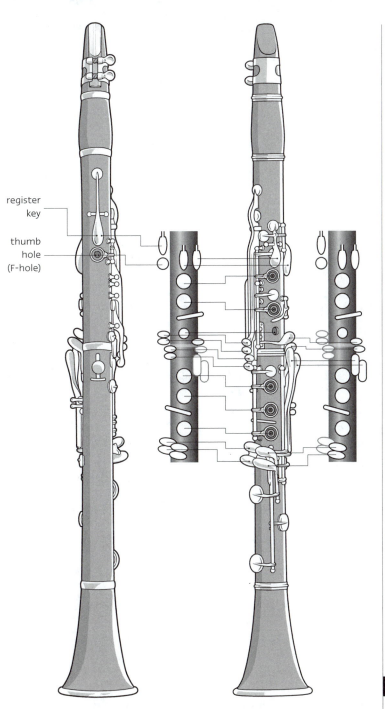

register
key

thumb
hole
(F-hole)

○ Don't press

● Press

E3 – F♭3

F3 – E♯3

F♯3 – G♭3

G3

218

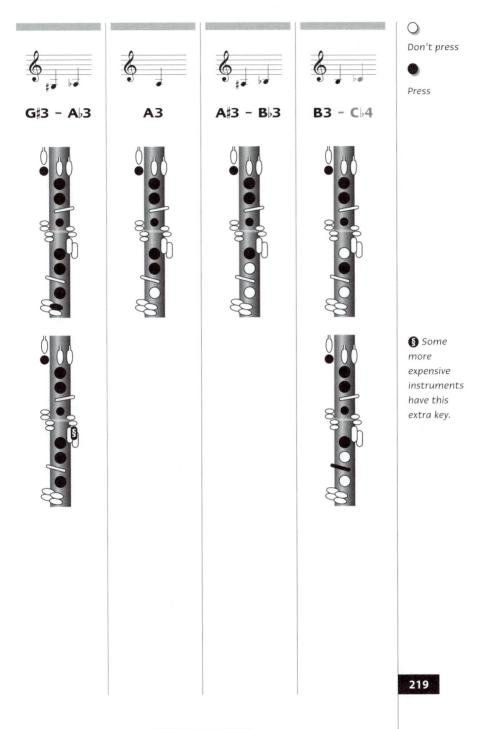

G#3 – A♭3

A3

A#3 – B♭3

B3 – C♭4

○ Don't press

● Press

§ Some more expensive instruments have this extra key.

219

Don't press ○

Press ●

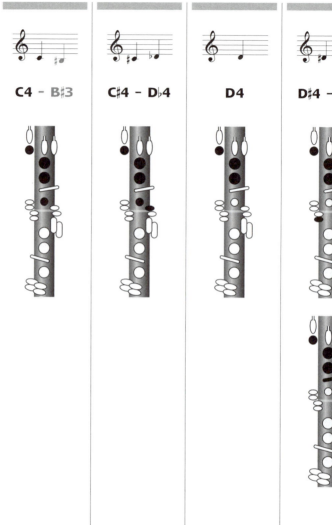

| C4 – B♯3 | C♯4 – D♭4 | D4 | D♯4 – E♭4 |

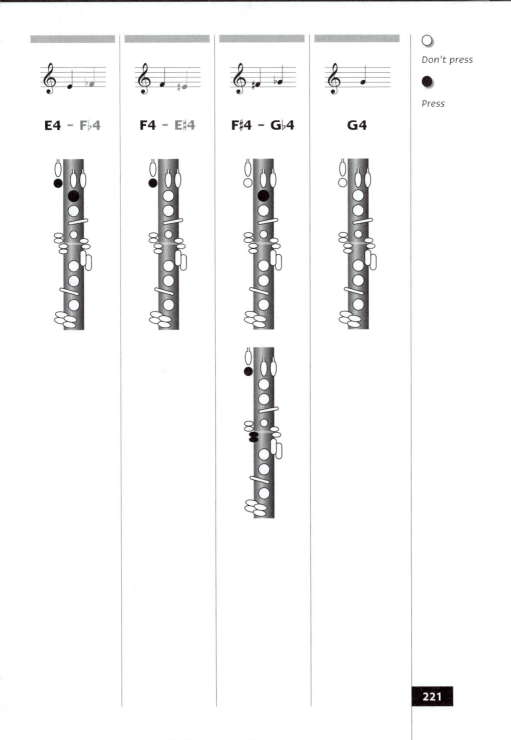

E4 – F♭4   F4 – E♯4   F♯4 – G♭4   G4

○ Don't press

● Press

Don't press

Press

G♯4 – A♭4	A4	A♯4 – B♭4	B4 – C♭5

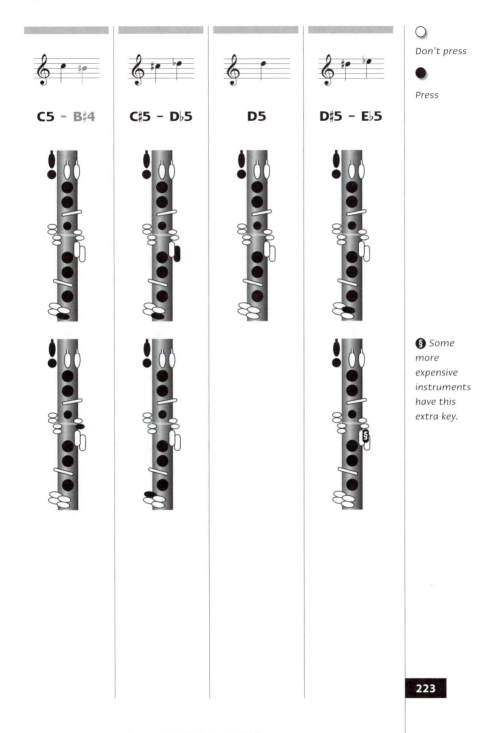

Don't press

Press

C5 – B♯4   **C♯5 – D♭5**   **D5**   **D♯5 – E♭5**

§ Some more expensive instruments have this extra key.

Don't press

Press

E5 – F♭5

F5 – E♯5

F♯5 – G♭5

G5

224

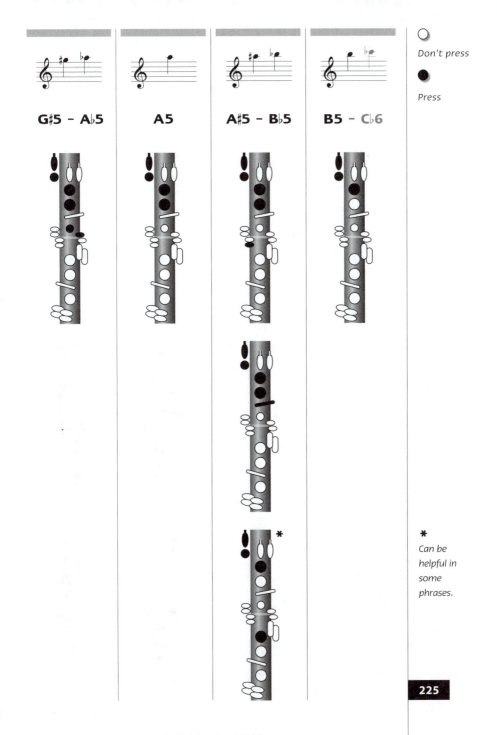

G♯5 – A♭5

A5

A♯5 – B♭5

B5 – C♭6

Don't press

Press

*
Can be
helpful in
some
phrases.

Don't press

Press

⊙ Improves
intonation.
Can be left
out in fast
phrases.

C5 – B♯4   **C♯6 – D♭6**   **D6**   **D♯6 – E♭6**

*
Can be
helpful in
some
phrases.

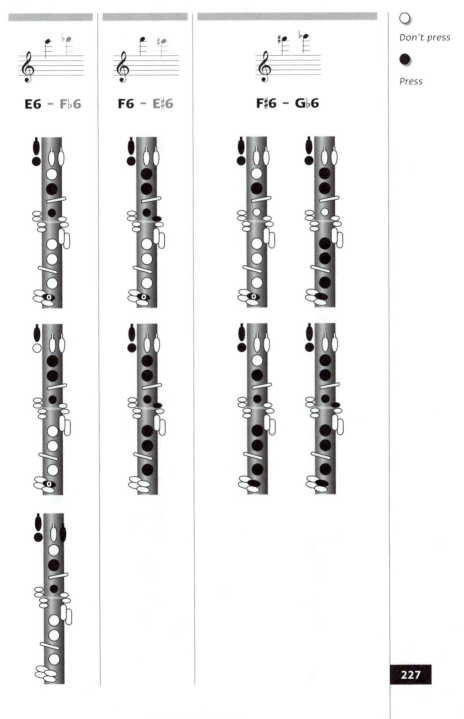

E6 – F♭6 F6 – E♯6 F♯6 – G♭6

Don't press

Press

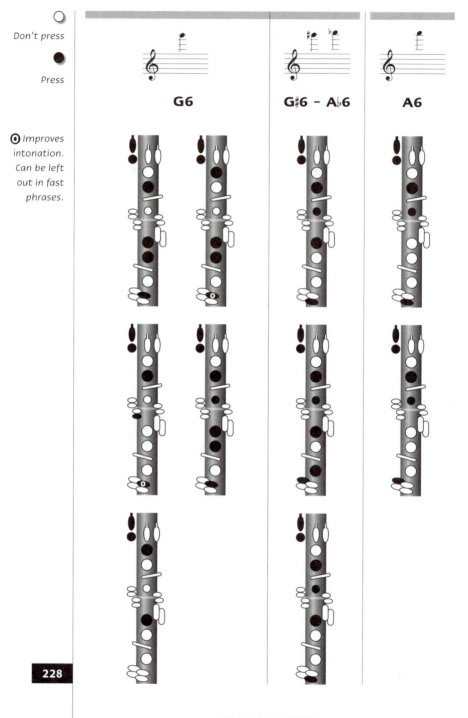

Don't press

Press

⊙ *Improves intonation. Can be left out in fast phrases.*

G6

G♯6 – A♭6

A6

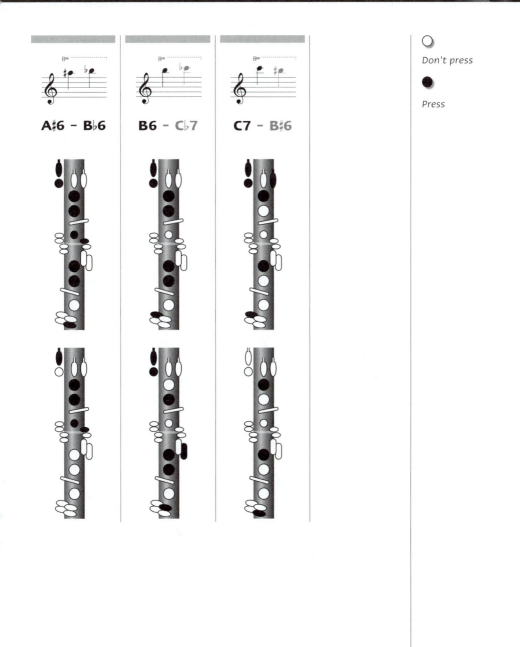

A♯6 – B♭6   B6 – C♭7   C7 – B♯6

○ Don't press

● Press

Essential Data

In the event that your instrument is stolen or lost, or if you decide to sell it, it's always useful to have all the relevant data close at hand. Jot down those details on the following pages. Whether for the insurance company, for the police, for the person who buys it or just for yourself.

INSURANCE

Company:

Phone: Website:

E-mail:

Agent:

Phone: Website:

E-mail:

Policy number: Premium:

INSTRUMENTS AND ACCESSORIES

Brand and type:

Serial number: Price:

Date of purchase:

Purchased from:

Phone: Website:

E-mail:

Brand and type:

Serial number: Price:

Date of purchase:

Purchased from:

Phone: Website:

E-mail:

Brand and type:

Serial number: Price:

Date of purchase:

Purchased from:

Phone: Website:

E-mail:

MOUTHPIECES

Brand and type:

Date of purchase: Price:

Purchased from:

Phone: Website:

E-mail:

Brand and type:

Date of purchase: Price:

Purchased from:

Phone: Website:

E-mail:

REEDS

Brand, type and number:

Price:

Comments:

Brand, type and number:

Price:

Comments:

Brand, type and number:

Price:

Comments:

Brand, type and number:

Price:

Comments:

ADDITIONAL NOTES

Index

Please check out the glossary on pages 203–208 for additional definitions of the terms used in this book.

233

The Tipbook Series

Did you like this Tipbook? There are also Tipbooks for your fellow band or orchestra members! The Tipbook Series features various books on musical instruments, including the singing voice, in addition to Tipbook Music on Paper, Tipbook Amplifiers and Effects, and Tipbook Music for Kids and Teens – a Guide for Parents.

Every Tipbook is a highly accessible and easy-to-read compilation of the knowledge and expertise of numerous musicians, teachers, technicians, and other experts, written for musicians of all ages, at all levels, and in any style of music. Please check www.tipbook.com for up to date information on the Tipbook Series!

All Tipbooks come with Tipcodes that offer additional information, sound files and short movies at www.tipbook.com

Instrument Tipbooks

All instrument Tipbooks offer a wealth of highly accessible, yet well-founded information on one or more closely related instruments. The first chapters of each Tipbook explain the very basics of the instrument(s), explaining all the parts and what they do, describing what's involved in learning to play, and indicating typical instrument prices. The core chapters, addressing advanced players as well, turn you into an instant expert on the instrument. This knowledge allows you to make an informed purchase and get the most out of your instrument. Comprehensive chapters on maintenance, intonation, and tuning are also included, as well a brief section on the history, the family, and the production of the instrument.

Tipbook Acoustic Guitar – $14.95

Tipbook Acoustic Guitar explains all of the elements that allow you to recognize and judge a guitar's timbre, performance, and playability, focusing on both steel-string and nylon-string instruments. There are chapters covering the various types of strings and their characteristics, and there's plenty of helpful information on changing and cleaning strings, on tuning and maintenance, and even on the care of your fingernails.

235

Tipbook Amplifiers and Effects – $14.99

Whether you need a guitar amp, a sound system, a multi-effects unit for a bass guitar, or a keyboard amplifier, *Tipbook Amplifiers and Effects* helps you to make a good choice. Two chapters explain general features (controls, equalizers, speakers, MIDI, etc.) and figures (watts, ohms, impedance, etc.), and further chapters cover the specifics of guitar amps, bass amps, keyboard amps, acoustic amps, and sound systems. Effects and effect units are dealt with in detail, and there are also chapters on microphones and pickups, and cables and wireless systems.

Tipbook Cello – $14.95

Cellists can find everything they need to know about their instrument in *Tipbook Cello*. The book gives you tips on how to select an instrument and choose a bow, tells you all about the various types of strings and rosins, and gives you helpful tips on the maintenance and tuning of your instrument. Basic information on electric cellos is included as well!

Tipbook Clarinet – $14.99

Tipbook Clarinet sheds light on every element of this fascinating instrument. The knowledge presented in this guide makes trying out and selecting a clarinet much easier, and it turns you into an instant expert on offset and in-line trill keys, rounded or French-style keys, and all other aspects of the instrument. Special chapters are devoted to reeds (selecting, testing, and adjusting reeds), mouthpieces and ligatures, and maintenance.

Tipbook Electric Guitar and Bass Guitar – $14.95

Electric guitars and bass guitars come in many shapes and sizes. *Tipbook Electric Guitar and Bass Guitar* explains all of their features and characteristics, from neck profiles, frets, and types of wood to different types of pickups, tuning machines, and — of course — strings. Tuning and advanced do-it-yourself intonation techniques are included.

Tipbook Drums – $14.95

A drum is a drum is a drum? Not true — and *Tipbook Drums* tells you all the ins and outs of their differences, from the type of wood to the dimensions of the shell, the shape of the bearing edge, and the drum's hardware. Special chapters discuss selecting drum sticks, drum heads, and cymbals. Tuning and muffling, two techniques a drummer must master to make the instrument sound as good as it can, are covered in detail, providing step-by-step instructions.

Tipbook Flute and Piccolo – $14.99

Flute prices range from a few hundred to fifty thousand dollars and more. *Tipbook Flute and Piccolo* tells you how workmanship, materials, and other elements make for different instruments with vastly different prices, and teaches you how to find the instrument that best suits your or your child's needs. Open-hole or closed-hole keys, a B-foot or a C-foot, split-E or donut, inline or offset G? You'll be able to answer all these questions — and more — after reading this guide.

Tipbook Keyboard and Digital Piano – $14.99

Buying a home keyboard or a digital piano may find you confronted with numerous unfamiliar terms. *Tipbook Keyboard and Digital Piano* explains all of them in a very easy-to-read fashion — from hammer action and non-weighted keys to MIDI, layers and splits, arpeggiators and sequencers, expression pedals and multi-switches, and more, including special chapters on how to judge the instrument's sound, accompaniment systems, and the various types of connections these instruments offer.

Tipbook Music for Kids and Teens – a Guide for Parents – $14.99

How do you inspire children to play music? How do you inspire them to practice? What can you do to help them select an instrument, to reduce stage fright, or to practice effectively? What can you do to make practice fun? How do you reduce sound levels and

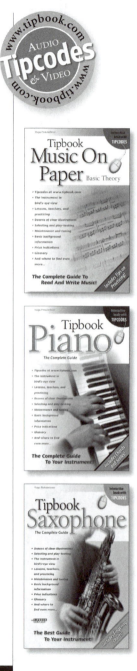

prevent hearing damage? These and many more questions are dealt with in *Tipbook Music for Kids and Teens – a Guide for Parents and Caregivers*. The book addresses all subjects related to the musical education of children from pre-birth to pre-adulthood.

Tipbook Music on Paper – $14.99

Tipbook Music on Paper – Basic Theory offers everything you need to read and understand the language of music. The book presumes no prior understanding of theory and begins with the basics, explaining standard notation, but moves on to advanced topics such as odd time signatures and transposing music in a fashion that makes things really easy to understand.

Tipbook Piano – $14.99

Choosing a piano becomes a lot easier with the knowledge provided in *Tipbook Piano*, which makes for a better understanding of this complex, expensive instrument without going into too much detail. How to judge and compare piano keyboards and pedals, the influence of the instrument's dimensions, different types of cabinets, how to judge an instrument's timbre, the difference between laminated and solid wood soundboards, accessories, hybrid and digital pianos, and why tuning and regulation are so important: Everything is covered in this handy guide.

Tipbook Saxophone – $14.95

At first glance, all alto saxophones look alike. And all tenor saxophones do too — yet they all play and sound different from each other. *Tipbook Saxophone* discusses the instrument in detail, explaining the key system and the use of additional keys, the different types of pads, corks, and springs, mouthpieces and how they influence timbre and playability, reeds (and how to select and adjust them) and much more. Fingering charts are also included!

Tipbook Trumpet and Trombone, Flugelhorn and Cornet – $14.99

The Tipbook on brass instruments focuses on the smaller horns listed in the title. It explains all of the jargon you come across when you're out to buy or rent an instrument, from bell material to the shape of the bore, the leadpipe, valves and valve slides, and all other elements of the horn. Mouthpieces, a crucial choice for the sound and playability of all brasswinds, are covered in a separate chapter.

Tipbook Violin and Viola – $14.95

Tipbook Violin and Viola covers a wide range of subjects, ranging from an explanation of different types of tuning pegs, fine tuners, and tailpieces, to how body dimensions and the bridge may influence the instrument's timbre. Tips on trying out instruments and bows are included. Special chapters are devoted to the characteristics of different types of strings, bows, and rosins, allowing you to get the most out of your instrument.

Tipbook Vocals – The Singing Voice – $14.95

Tipbook Vocals –The Singing Voice helps you realize the full potential of your singing voice. The book, written in close collaboration with classical and non-classical singers and teachers, allows you to discover the world's most personal and precious instrument without reminding you of anatomy class. Topics include breathing and breath support, singing loudly without hurting your voice, singing in tune, the timbre of your voice, articulation, registers and ranges, memorizing lyrics, and more. The main purpose of the chapter on voice care is to prevent problems.

International editions

The Tipbook Series is also available in Spanish, French, German, Dutch, Italian, and Chinese. For more information, please visit us at www.tipbook.com.

Tipbook Series Music and Musical Instruments

Tipbook Acoustic Guitar
ISBN 978-1-4234-4275-2, HL00332373 — $14.95

Tipbook Amplifiers and Effects
ISBN 978-1-4234-6277-4, HL00332776 — $14.99

Tipbook Cello
ISBN 978-1-4234-5623-0, HL00331904 — $14.95

Tipbook Clarinet
ISBN 978-1-4234-6524-9, HL00332803 — $14.99

Tipbook Drums
ISBN 978-90-8767-102-0, HL00331474 — $14.95

Tipbook Electric Guitar and Bass Guitar
ISBN 978-1-4234-4274-5, HL00332372 — $14.95

Tipbook Flute and Piccolo
ISBN 978-1-4234-6525-6, HL00332804 — $14.99

Tipbook Home Keyboard and Digital Piano
ISBN 978-1-4234-4277-6, HL00332375 — $14.99

Tipbook Music for Kids and Teens
ISBN 978-1-4234-6526-3, HL00332805 — $14.99

Tipbook Music on Paper — Basic Theory
ISBN 978-1-4234-6529-4, HL00332807 — $14.99

Tipbook Piano
ISBN 978-1-4234-6278-1, HL00332777 — $14.99

Tipbook Saxophone
ISBN 978-90-8767-101-3, HL00331475 — $14.95

Tipbook Trumpet and Trombone, Flugelhorn and Cornet
ISBN 978-1-4234-6527-0, HL00332806 — $14.99

Tipbook Violin and Viola
ISBN 978-1-4234-4276-9, HL00332374 — $14.95

Tipbook Vocals — The Singing Voice
ISBN 978-1-4234-5622-3, HL00331949 — $14.95

Check www.tipbook.com for additional information!